LIFE-CHANGING ECONOMICS
OF DISRUPTIVE TECHNOLOGIES

TECHONOMICS
YOU SHOULD KNOW

LIFE-CHANGING ECONOMICS
OF DISRUPTIVE TECHNOLOGIES

TECHONOMICS
YOU SHOULD KNOW

TAOSHA WANG

ISBN 979-8-86-141138-7

First Edition

10 9 8 7 6 5 4 3 2 1

To Dana

PART I

INTRODUCTION

With headlines about artificial intelligence, virtual reality, and blockchain technologies popping up at every corner, it feels like civilization is on the cusp of a major breakthrough. We are excited about the seemingly endless possibilities of these technologies, but anxious about how they may affect the way we live and work. We marvel at how powerful they are yet feel uneasy about how influential the small group of individuals controlling these technologies may be. We have witnessed crypto billionaires rising at dizzying speeds and digital art fetching eye-watering prices but are still unsure whether we should partake in these brand-new concepts of money and valuables. How exactly do these disruptive technologies work? How will they affect our economic well-being? Will we lose our jobs? Will we still make decent earnings? Will we be lucky enough to identify once-in-a-lifetime opportunities to earn great wealth?

Fortunately, while the next generation of technologies is constantly moving and hard to predict, the economic framework that studies the impact of these technologies is well established. Humans are profoundly economic beings, and our actions are bound by a consistent set of principles like rationality and self-interest. As individuals, we maximize our economic benefits and minimize our economic costs when we pursue job opportunities, develop new skills, and make money decisions. Collectively, economic factors such as how productive we are, how output is distributed, and how wealth accumulates over time shape our social structure and our relationships with one another.

The study of economics addresses three main questions: what do we produce, how do we produce them, and how are we rewarded for the production? In this book, we will examine the answers to these questions in light of the latest technologies. We call this interplay between technology and economics *techonomics*. We will delineate the eighteen techonomic impacts that are most relevant to our real lives through jobs, income, or wealth. These include a quantitative assessment of AI's impact on the job market and a review of the likelihood of mass unemployment. We will reveal an inherent flaw in AI design that makes it unfit to replace humans for many tasks. We will discuss the aggregate economic impact of using new technologies to get more done for less and how this affects our relative income levels. We will touch on innovative forms of wealth that have been enabled by the new technologies, such as whether digital assets and money are real.

The future is already here—it's just not very evenly distributed. We are already living with bits and pieces of the future, with much more to come. Corporations have already started adopting AI into their daily business practices. Central banks and large financial institutions are already using blockchain technologies to facilitate transactions and manage money. Trendsetting artists are already performing to massive interactive audiences in the virtual space. By relying on economic theories that hold true over time, we can more clearly see how our future may change through the iterations of new technologies.

This book is not a user manual on the latest AI technologies. It is not a trading guide on what crypto-currencies to buy. It does not attempt to project a static image of the future, whether it be living in a digital oasis like in *Ready Player One* or floating leglessly in cartoonish conference rooms per Meta's commercial pitch.

This book will instead offer a framework for the economic impacts of today's disruptive technologies. It will hopefully provide clarity on the economic horizon of the next few decades, which is a time frame relevant for us and our children. This book is intended for people whose fields of work may see greater adoption of AI, mixed reality, and blockchain technologies; who wonder how best to prepare themselves and their children for the challenges and opportunities ahead; and who contemplate the best path forward for human civilization as we navigate the uncertainties together. The decision to adopt the myriad of disruptive technologies and in what fashion should not rest in the hands of a few tech billionaires or big corporations. It should be up to the hundreds of millions of potential users of these technologies and billions of people whose lives may be impacted. It is therefore imperative that we equip ourselves with knowledge on these issues. So let us embark on this journey to explore the economic impact of some of the greatest technological advancements of our time.

INTRODUCTION

CHAPTER **1**

TODAY'S DISRUPTIVE TECHNOLOGIES

We identify artificial intelligence, virtual and mixed reality, and blockchain technologies as the three main examples of today's disruptive technologies. These technologies have had major breakthroughs that have garnered widespread public attention. There have been significant investments in these areas, and more are certainly coming down the pipeline. These will unleash more powerful potential in these rapidly moving technologies. They have already made their commercial debut and found some success in real-life use cases. They can be adopted on a much wider basis, which can unlock a high commercial value.

ARTIFICIAL INTELLIGENCE

Artificial intelligence is a general term that describes machines that behave like human beings. These humanlike behaviors include the ability to reason, learn, plan, and generate ideas and content.

The concept of artificial intelligence, or AI, has existed for decades. In 1950, Alan Turing, an English mathematician and philosopher, published a paper called "Computing Machinery and Intelligence," which discusses the question of whether machines can think. The paper proposed a test on machine intelligence. Now widely known as the Turing Test, it states that a machine can be considered intelligent if, from the perspective of another human, it can exhibit behavior that is indistinguishable from human behaviors. In 1997, Deep Blue, a chess-playing computer program developed by IBM, became an international sensation. Deep Blue played against the reigning world champion and won in an undisputed manner. This victory was considered a milestone in the history of artificial intelligence. The development of smartphone technologies brought artificial intelligence closer to average users. In 2011, Apple released the first iPhones equipped with Siri, a voice-controlled AI assistant. Siri supports a wide range of commands, such as making calls, setting alarms, scheduling events, and interacting with various apps. Over five hundred million customers use Siri, according to Apple. In 2022, OpenAI, an American AI research lab partially owned by Microsoft, launched the AI chatbot ChatGPT to the general public. ChatGPT became the most quickly adopted modern technology, which marks a watershed moment in AI development.

AI is a broad concept. Anything from Siri to ChatGPT to the bloodthirsty robots depicted in sci-fi movies can be considered AI. Machine learning is a school within AI in which machines, without explicit instruction, learn and act on information to improve their performance over time. Within machine learning, deep learning is a prominent subset that uses multiple hidden layers of artificial neutral networks to learn from the last amount of data. The design of deep learning is inspired by the way human brains function. The type of AI that has captured the world's attention is generative AI, such as ChatGPT, which belongs to the deep learning school of AI.

Generative AI is a type of AI that can generate new content by studying historical data. Compared with previous generations, the latest generative AI technology is unique in three main aspects.

First, it is multipurpose. Generative AI can write essays, paint pictures, summarize long essays, engage in humanlike conversation, translate, make new proposals, explain a joke, and the list goes on. It exhibits a "general" level of intelligence and competence. OpenAI's ChatGPT has even scored near the ninetieth percentile in standardized tests for undergraduate and graduate school admissions, such as the SAT and GRE.

Second, it is easy to access. Commands are given in simple prompts, which are text and images fed to AI to elicit their responses. This allows users without any coding skills to use them, thus making them accessible to the general public.

Third, generative AI has seen an unprecedented rate of adoption. It took ChatGPT merely two months after its initial launch to reach one hundred million users, which is by far the fastest in modern technology. To reach the same number of users, it took the telephones seventy-five years, the World Wide Web seven years, and Instagram almost three years.

The Way Humans Think

To understand how AI can be used, we should first understand how humans and machines think differently. Let's start with humans.

In 1637, French philosopher René Descartes declared "I think, therefore I am" as the first principle of his philosophy. Over the subsequent centuries, this statement became a foundational element for western philosophy. It removes the fundamental doubt of existence by asserting that the very act of doubting existence proves we exist. Our ability to think defines who we are.

Human beings are good at processing chains of logical causality. We are able to draw conclusions on issues we have not yet observed from facts that we already know are true. By building our arguments upon sound reasons, we can often convince ourselves that the conclusion reached at the end of a long chain of logic is valid. The simplified form of a logical chain is: "If A, then B; if B, then C; if C, then D," and thus, "If A, then D." If we truly understand something, we understand why certain inputs will always produce the same output. We are not guessing around for an approximate answer; we know, in a deterministic way, the answer because we understand the reasons behind it.

Humans start training for the ability to reason early. Between the ages of two and three years, human babies start asking the "why" question as they try to establish the causal relationships between things. They start to make countless logical links of "if A, then B" in their brains. If they are hungry, then they must eat. If they don't brush their teeth before bed, then they will have cavities. Research shows that a child of four to six years of age will ask an average of about four hundred questions per day. While these questions, ranging from "Why can't we get a puppy?" to "Why is the sky blue?" can be a real test of a parent's patience, they mark an important milestone in a child's cognitive development. Asking why is an intrinsically human impulse to understand the reasons behind various observed phenomena. It is a way for human brains to establish chains of causality, which are the foundation of logical thinking.

The Way AI Thinks

Unlike humans, who are able to reason logically, AIs are fundamentally statistical models. They come up with answers to our questions by solving complicated math. The prevailing deep-learning AI models work in two stages. The first stage is training, which is when the machine goes through large amounts of data to establish the statistical relationships between input and output. The second stage is inference, which is when machines are put to work by making predictions of output based on new input given.

To understand how AI models work, consider a simple image recognition model, which is trained to identify animal species. The model is trained using a large set of existing data consisting of many animal pictures and their corresponding species labels. The model establishes hidden layers of data nodes that connect input and output. The job of these data nodes is to assign different weights to different attributes. The higher the weight, the more relevant the attribute is in driving the final output. For example, the background color of the puppy image could be an attribute, but it would not be important for determining the species of the animal. Meanwhile, the shape of the puppy's ears would be a more important attribute. In today's deep-learning models, these attributes are so complicated and granular that they are not visible to any outside observers, including the engineers who train the models, so we do not know exactly what factors the machines find important and why. Once these nodes and weights are established in the training stage, a new input (i.e., another puppy image) can be passed through the model for prediction. The AI converts the image pixels into numerical values and looks for similar patterns from its training data set. The image model is likely to suggest that the puppy has a high probability of being a dog because the numerical values generated from the pixels of the puppy image share more relevant similarities with the dog pictures used in the training process than with any other species.

A fundamental characteristic of AI is that it does not "understand" the problems it tries to solve. This gives rise to its inherent flaw, known as hallucination. When solving a question, AI does not attempt to give the logically correct answer but instead guesses what answer most "looks like" the correct answer. As statistical models, AI makes predictions by solving for best fit with training data. This is different from the deterministic logic of humans, in which the same input always produces the same output following the same logic. This inherently statistical nature gives rise to the hallucination problem, which is when generative AI confidently produces answers that are either incomplete or outright wrong. For example, many users of AI image generators have found that the machines do a particularly poor job at drawing human hands. The AI would produce vivid skin textures and a convincing overall shape, but an extra finger or two often stick out from the wrong side of the palm. This happens because the AI does not know, through deterministic logic, that a normal human hand always has four fingers and one opposing thumb. It has merely generated an image, through statistical association, that "looks like" the actual human hands. In other words, AI is trained for the confidence with which it spits out information but not the accuracy of the information.

Despite its inherent flaws, AI can surprise us positively with what it can do. Studies have shown that very large AI models develop more generalized abilities in a sudden and often unexpected manner. Researchers call this phenomenon the "emergent" behaviors of AI. For example, when a large language AI model, which is trained to only perform language tasks, crosses a certain size threshold, its arithmetic capabilities sharply and disproportionally improve. In other words, AIs seem to become suddenly a lot "smarter" once they reach a certain size. The intuitive explanation of this phenomenon is that language is an embodiment of general knowledge. Therefore, AI models trained on sufficient language data have effectively been trained on expressions of general knowledge too. The model that can predict that "two" is the best contextual finish to a sentence starting with "one plus one equals" is effectively doing math.

The emergent behavior of very large AI models explains why AIs are getting bigger and more complex and, as a result, more expensive to train. The size and the complexity of AI models are measured by the number of parameters or variables in the AI model whose values are adjusted during training. The more parameters there are, the more detailed the statistical calculations and the more accurate its predictions will be. In 2020, OpenAI released its GPT-3 model, the basis of chatbot ChatGPT, which was trained on 175 billion parameters. In 2021, Google Brain unveiled another AI model with 1.6 trillion parameters—nine times as large as the GPT-3 model. Various organizations are racing to train the next biggest AI models because they want to be positively surprised. OpenAI's latest GPT-4 model reportedly cost over US$100 million to train and has nearly two trillion parameters.

AI has already been adopted in many real-life scenarios. The recommendation algorithm behind YouTube that keeps us glued to our screens for hours is powered by AI. The chatbot that takes your order at a drive-through restaurant is powered by AI. The creative industry is rapidly incorporating generative AI tools into its existing content creation process. As more businesses and individuals incorporate AI into their productive activities, it will have a lot more room to grow its application scenarios.

VIRTUAL REALITY AND MIXED REALITY

Virtual reality (VR) is a simulated experience that enables users to explore the virtual world in an immersive manner. Most VR technologies today use headsets to generate sensory stimulations in a virtual environment. One of the most popular VR devices is the Oculus series of headsets. The headset features a head-mounted centerpiece paired with two handheld controllers. The gadget weighs a little over one pound and costs US$500 at retail price. Its manufacturer, Oculus VR, became part of Facebook following an acquisition in 2014, and the Oculus Rift headset made its commercial debut in 2016.

Mixed reality, sometimes called augmented reality, is similar to VR and shares a lot of the underlying technologies. Instead of creating a fully immersive digital experience, mixed reality devices allow an interactive experience that combines the real world and the computer-generated digital world. Mixed reality technologies gained mainstream popularity from the hit mobile game Pokémon Go. Players use their mobile phones to create digital avatars, move across real-world surroundings, and capture virtual Pokémon, which appear in real-world locations at certain times per game design. In 2023, Apple announced its mixed reality headset called Apple Vision Pro, which the company advertised as a "spatial computer." The headset, which can switch between a fully immersive mode and a transparency mode that allows eye contact with the environment, retails for US$3,499 and is expected to be released in early 2024.

The COVID-19 pandemic has greatly accelerated the adoption of virtual and remote technologies. As lockdowns forced people around the world to reorganize the way they conduct businesses and daily activities, society started to embrace remote and virtual technologies as a structural shift rather than a temporary solution to the pandemic problem. Companies issued more flexible work-from-home policies, workers purchased new computers to refresh their home office, and families upgraded their home entertainment equipment.

Virtual and remote technologies have enabled successful digitalization of traditionally in-person events such as concerts. During the pandemic in April 2020, Travis Scott, an American rapper, performed a nine-minute virtual concert online in Fortnite. Fortnite is a highly popular online video game where large numbers of players fight to be the last person standing in an open-world environment. Travis Scott's virtual concert ran for two nights in a row and attracted a total of twelve million live participants and another 120 million views of the event recording. The concert kicked off with a surprise. Instead of the artist making a regular entrance onto the virtual performance stage, a giant planet shot down from the Fortnite sky. The planet was half hollow with a stereo speaker at its core, roller-coasters on its surface, and a bright satellite orbiting its perimeter. Against this background, a two-hundred-foot-tall version of Travis Scott launched right into the game scene, Godzilla style. Fortnite players bounced, danced, and floated as the rapper teleported from one spot in the game map to another, at times lifting the entire audience with a virtual hand gesture. In the background, the sky rained fire, and thunderstorms crashed with kaleidoscopic light effects.

The unlimited reach of the virtual sphere can bring about a tremendous economy of scale. The largest stadiums in the United States can host no more than 110,000 people when fully sold out. A larger concert requires more advanced equipment and more complicated security systems and often creates more logistical stress for the local communities. In other words, as in-person events become bigger, they become exponentially more difficult to manage. The virtual reality event has no capacity limit. Graphic effects and sound quality do not diminish, whether you are the first person to attend or the twelve-millionth. The view of the stage does not get blocked by the people standing in front of you bobbing their heads. And you do not have to worry about paying an outrageous price to the ticket scalpers because the limited number of good seats are sold out. The two-night Travis Scott x Fortnite event reportedly grossed $20 million, which is a phenomenal figure. The physical tour by the same artist, which included more than fifty concerts over a four-month period, grossed $53.5 million.

Virtual events can create visual and aesthetic experiences that are far superior to what is possible in the physical world. In other words, a virtual experience does not have to be an inferior imitation of the real-world experience. The Fortnite performance was record breaking not just in commercial terms but also in its otherworldly effects that have been uniquely enabled by the virtual technologies. Many who participated live said the event was even better than a physical concert. Some gamers said they "will never forget the hype and chills." The surreally beautiful graphics, the experience of a massive crowd, and movements that defied the laws of physics could only exist in a virtual space. These brand-new sensory experiences evoked strong emotions that physical experiences would not have been able to match up to.

The virtual world will become fuller and more engaging, which will change the way we live and work. Tech giants are making big bets, building out infrastructures that will facilitate the virtual world where we can interact with each other, share experiences, and build things in a digital space. Mark Zuckerberg thought this place should be called the metaverse. Besides renaming itself Meta, his company also plans to invest over US$100 billion in this line of business over the next few years. In summer 2023, Apple joined Meta in making a big bet on virtual and mixed reality by introducing the Vision Pro headset. Apple has a track record of getting us to buy things we did not even know we needed or liked (think iPad or AirPods) and changing our consumer behavior for good. As more investments are made in this area and new products become available, virtual and mixed reality technologies will change the way we conduct work activities, entertain ourselves, and socialize with others.

BLOCKCHAIN, CRYPTOCURRENCIES, AND DIGITAL ASSETS

In 2008, Satoshi Nakamoto, a cryptographer whose true identity remains unknown, created the Bitcoin blockchain as an open-source software. The Bitcoin blockchain is a public ledger that records all Bitcoin transactions. New bitcoins are issued as a reward for creating new blocks, a bookkeeping effort, on the blockchain. This event marked the birth of both blockchain technology (a decentralized method of account keeping) and Bitcoin (the first crypto-currency). Under the Bitcoin protocol, a new block containing Bitcoin transactions is added every ten minutes to the existing chain of transaction records, and a predetermined number of new bitcoins are created as a reward for keeping such records. Every four years, the reward, measured in the new number of bitcoins issued for adding a new block, is automatically reduced by half based on the design algorithm.

Since its launch more than a decade ago, Bitcoin has become the oldest and most valuable cryptocurrency. It has a current market cap of over US$400 billion. Bitcoin has inspired the creation of various other blockchains and related digital currencies and assets.

Bitcoin: Digital Gold on Blockchain?

Bitcoin has often been referred to as the gold of the digital age. An important reason for this analogy is that the total supply of both bitcoin and gold is capped. The world's total supply of gold is determined by the amount of naturally occurring atomic deposits on Earth. The total supply of bitcoin is also capped by a mathematical algorithm designed by its creator. Because the speed at which new bitcoins are minted halves every four years, fewer and fewer new bitcoins will be issued until eventually no new bitcoins will be created. Mathematically, Bitcoin will reach its supply limit of twenty-one million units on October 5, 2138.

Gold has occupied a special place in human society for a long time. For thousands of years, it has been a symbol of wealth and a nearly universally accepted means of wealth exchange. The world's major currencies such as the US dollar used to have their value linked to gold at a fixed exchange ratio to evoke public confidence in paper money during war times. Today, gold is still widely held by central banks around the world as a reserve asset to back up the value of their local currencies. A vast amount of wealth is stored in gold. The total physical gold that has been mined in the world is worth more than US$10 trillion based on the latest gold price. In addition to its physical form, gold is a liquid financial instrument whose value is affected by investor appetite changing in different market conditions.

Bitcoin, meanwhile, has existed for less than twenty years. Its market value is only a fraction of gold, and it is not nearly as universally accepted. Nonetheless, Bitcoin is the most widely held and frequently traded cryptocurrency. For people who are converting their fiat money like the US dollar or Japanese yen into cryptocurrencies for the first time, Bitcoin is usually the first choice. Many people who buy Bitcoin may not necessarily be experts in the underlying blockchain technologies. They nonetheless choose to buy it as a way to diversify money investments and participate in the potential upside of the related technologies.

Smart Contracts and Digital Assets

Debuted in 2013, Ethereum is currently the second-most-valuable cryptocurrency. Similar to Bitcoin, it is also a decentralized, open-source blockchain software. Unlike Bitcoin, it has the additional feature of embedded smart contracts.

The smart contract is an extremely important feature for the application of blockchain technology. It automates the enforcement of predetermined agreements, removes the need for both parties to trust each other, and eliminates the need for a third party to mediate. In other words, smart contracts are agreements that execute themselves.

A key application of the smart contract is its ability to assign ownership and enforce the transferability of nonfungible tokens, or NFTs. NFTs are unique digital objects that are recorded on blockchains. Unlike cryptocurrencies, which are fungible (i.e., one bitcoin is always the same as the next bitcoin), NFTs are noninterchangeable. So far, the most common use case of NFTs is to store digital art, which allows the lineage of the art piece to be fully tracked from creation to every transfer of ownership. The Ethereum blockchain is home to most of the smart contracts and NFTs today. In the context of blockchain technologies, cryptocurrencies, and NFTs are collectively referred to as digital assets.

Over the last decade, blockchain technology, crypto-currencies, and NFTs have blossomed from novel concepts to technologies that have exerted real impacts on the mainstream financial world. Large financial institutions are looking to harness the power of this decentralization technology. JPMorgan, for example, established a blockchain-based platform, Onyx, to facilitate wholesale payment transactions. Central banks have taken note of blockchain technologies and are exploring digital currencies to improve transaction efficiency and security. According to the World Economic Forum, over one hundred countries, representing more than 95% of world GDP, are actively engaging in research, development, pilots, or execution of central bank digital currencies. The Chinese central bank has debuted its digital Renminbi, the local currency, for public testing in 2021. The European Central Bank is investigating whether a digital euro should be introduced.

Some early adopters of blockchain technologies have been well rewarded financially. Over the last ten years, the value of Bitcoin against that of the US dollar has increased by over two hundred times. In 2021, a piece of NFT artwork titled *The Merge* fetched a sale of US$91.8 million, which became the new record for the most expensive artwork sold publicly by a living artist. The identity of the artist, working under the pseudonym Pak, remains unknown. In 2022, nineteen blockchain and crypto billionaires made it to Forbes's World's Billionaires List.

Blockchain technology and digital assets already serve multifaceted roles in our lives. They represent a utility function that records financial transactions on blockchains in a decentralized way. They provide destinations for diversified personal investments. We may hold cryptocurrencies for their potential to appreciate against our home currency. We may hold NFT digital art as a form of luxury spending or unconventional investment. As the technologies become more mature, they will find more interactions with our lives.

CHAPTER **2**

LIFE-RELEVANT
ECONOMIC QUESTIONS

Our economic lives are an important pillar in defining who we are and how we live. They determine how we spend a big chunk of our waking hours, what kind of life we can afford for ourselves and our family, and often our relationships with others.

The study of economics attempts to answer three basic questions: what should we produce, how should we produce them, and how should we be rewarded for our productive activities? These three questions can serve as a framework to examine the different aspects of our economic lives and how they are being affected by today's disruptive technology.

WHAT DO WE PRODUCE?

An average private sector employee in the United States works thirty-four hours per week according to the Bureau of Labor Statistics. This means nearly half of our waking weekday hours are spent at work. Many of us spend more time there than with our families or friends on a regular basis.

What we produce defines our profession. A pianist performs music to be enjoyed as a form of entertainment. A salesperson engages potential buyers and matches their needs with the right products. An engineer solves problems by designing and maintaining either physical machines or software systems. Our professions often give us a sense of identity and purpose in life. Jobs like medical doctors are often viewed as prestigious and imply a higher level of education, income, and social status for the practitioners. Japanese culture celebrates the mastering of one's profession and has coined the term *shokunin*, translated literally as *craftsman*, which describes a professional who delivers the best professional quality out of social and moral obligations and takes immense pride in doing so.

Choosing a profession is an important decision both for individuals and society as a whole. Many white-collar jobs have decade-long career progression paths that often start with a focused area of undergraduate study. After they enter the workforce, workers continue to develop specialized skills and establish interpersonal relationships, so they rarely take jumping into another unrelated field lightly. At an aggregate level, a person's loyalty to their respective career path can create a structural mismatch between the supply of workers who spend decades developing certain skills and the demand of companies who are responding to the latest technological changes. In 2021, a study by the French government suggested that 29% of French working individuals had an apparent skill mismatch with their occupations. Skill mismatch at such scale is problematic for a few reasons. Workers receive substantially lower wages than if they had been in the right job. Workers are less fulfilled by completing tasks that are not in their best interest or qualification. A structural shortage of labor makes it difficult for companies to hire the right person and thwarts overall economic growth.

We plan an educational path for ourselves and our children, hoping for the best job prospects. How certain skills or educations are valued has a lot to do with the socioeconomic structure and prevailing technologies of our society. The extraordinary success of the technology sector and the seemingly boundless power of programmers who become self-made billionaires have sent many students into computer science classrooms. In some places, software coding classes are offered to children as young as five years old, before they even learn primary school math. These educational offerings tap into the eagerness and anxiety of parents who want to ensure their children are equipped with the skills of the future.

How Do New Technologies Change What We Produce?

In 2011, Marc Andreessen, a venture capitalist, declared that "software is eating the world." He elaborates that all the major sectors are experiencing severe disruptions from software. The biggest bookseller? Amazon, a software company. The largest direct marketing platform? Google, a software company. The fastest-growing telecom company? Skype, a software company. The phenomenal rise of the software industry in the following decade proved that Mr. Andreessen was a visionary. The humbly dressed programmers working from their parents' garages have disrupted one industry after another, creating immense fortunes while doing so. As a result, software engineers are among the most sought-after professions in the US, commanding one of the highest salaries.

Today's generative AIs have the potential to disrupt many job tasks that have so far been performed mostly by humans. AI can write a business memo, create a portrait, summarize a book, and plan a trip with uncanny efficiency. The low-hanging fruit for commercial applications of AI technology includes customer service, where machines are already capable of informative and natural interactions, as well as content creation, where machines can generate fluid pieces of poems and images based on simple prompts. These job tasks require AI to act "like humans." At the same time, they do not require a very high level of accuracy, so the risk of AI hallucination is manageable. For jobs that require a higher level of accuracy, AI may be able to assist human professionals in sifting through large amounts of data and take up the more repetitive portion of their daily responsibilities.

While old jobs may go away, new career opportunities and career paths are being created. Only a few months after generative AI made its consumer debut, a new profession called "prompt engineer," whose job is to pose questions for AI to improve their answers, became highly in demand. As companies look for ways to deploy AI technology, they need prompt engineers to implement it effectively within their company infrastructure. The prompt engineer role does not require a programming background and pays generous salaries ranging between US$300,000 and US$400,000. As new technologies iterate, future generations of professionals may spend fewer years under the apprenticeship of senior colleagues before they are given more responsibilities. Future technologies, like generative AI, are likely to be easy to use, multifunctional, and rapidly evolving. The notion that a career path may take decades with a large share of the reward reaped in the later part of the path may one day become preposterous, given how quickly the underlying technologies are changing.

HOW DO WE PRODUCE?

The way we produce has a direct impact on our relationships with our jobs and determines whether we have fulfilling careers or dread the morning alarms. The nature of this relationship has changed dramatically over time. Working in a nineteenth-century factory in Europe, for example, often meant ten to twelve hours a day spent in hazardous working conditions. The suffering of these factory workers inspired Karl Marx, a German philosopher, to develop his theory on alienation, which describes how workers become more estranged from their human nature when they spend long hours working jobs that are dreary and repetitive out of economic necessity. Marx should be surprised to learn that in twenty-first-century Silicon Valley, free lunches are considered office staples. Many offices are equipped with amenities such as pool tables and arcade rooms. Google popularized the concept of the "20% rule," where employees are encouraged to spend 20% of their time working on whatever they think will benefit the company. This empowers the employees to take more ownership and be more creative.

For much of our economic history, capital and labor have been the two primary resources for economic activities, and there was a clear divide between the two. Capital is used to secure the critical physical inputs needed for the prevailing mode of economic production, which includes everything from raw materials and equipment to land. Labor, often referred to as employees or human capital, works hand in hand with the physical capital resources. Humans build, operate, and maintain machines while machines perform the specific instructions humans have given to them.

How Do New Technologies Change the Way We Produce?

The relationship between capital and labor, or between machines and humans, has become more intertwined. Today's machines can make recommendations to humans and influence our behaviors. AI specialized in medical imaging can detect anomalies that are too fine for human eyes to see, and their findings make it possible for human doctors to diagnose and treat diseases earlier. Machines can be a creative partner for human beings. With a few simple prompts, they can produce uncanny imagery and help artists visualize scenes that were once only in their heads.

New technologies also allow us to work in more flexible manners that better suit our needs. An effective working team in the future can be a lot smaller than it is today. AI technology is a productivity-boosting tool that helps people achieve a lot more than before. One person assisted by AI may possess a lot more "brain" power than a traditional multi-person team because AI is able to sift through a large amount of information and present it in an easy-to-digest fashion. On the other hand, an effective working team in the future can also be a lot bigger than it is today. The smart contract feature in blockchain technology can be an effective workflow management tool, automating the process of allocating tasks, monitoring progress, and distributing rewards. This can significantly reduce the hassle of coordinating a large team and accelerate the overall workflow by limiting downtime. Virtual and mixed reality tools may make remote interactions feel more in person and effective. Accenture is an IT consulting firm that helps many companies implement the latest technologies into their business practices. The company employs over seven hundred thousand people worldwide. Forty percent of this very large work force is based in India, serving clients from all over the world and generating nearly 50% of their revenue from across the Pacific Ocean in North America.

Workers in the future will need to be able to deploy the latest technologies in a responsible way. Disruptive technologies can upend the way we do things before the necessary checks and balances are established. Shortly after ChatGPT launched, several scientific papers were published listing ChatGPT as a coauthor. However, leading science journals soon banned ChatGPT co-authorship because the AI chatbot cannot be held responsible for its hallucination risk. Without understanding the limits of the new tool they deploy, researchers risk publishing scientifically inaccurate content and tarnishing their academic reputation. The early Facebook motto of "move fast and break things" is certainly unsuitable in this case.

HOW ARE WE REWARDED?

Earning a salary or wage is the way most workers are rewarded for their work. Beyond fixed salaries and wages, white-collar employees today often receive additional income, such as stock-based compensation and performance-based bonuses. These are effective ways to align the economic incentives of employees with their employers. For example, when a company decides to reduce worker headcounts, which would save costs and boost profitability, the company's stock prices are likely to rise. Typically, employees should object to this plan for fear of losing their jobs. However, employees who know they can retain their jobs will benefit from higher company share prices and are likely to be supportive of the plan. In other words, wage earners may not find agreement among themselves on key job-related issues. Some employees may even object to better workplace amenities on the grounds that it will reduce the profits of their company shares. In addition to stocks and bonuses, companies in the blockchain technology business may also offer cryptocurrencies as rewards for their employees. The value of these cryptocurrencies increases when the underlying blockchain technology becomes more widely adopted or when there is more speculative interest.

How Do New Technologies Change the Way We Are Rewarded?

Today's disruptive technologies are enabling employers to save wage costs in innovative ways. AI software will perform more responsibilities that used to be conducted by humans. Jobs paying higher wages in certain parts of the world may be reallocated to other regions with lower income levels. At an aggregate level, companies can spend less on wage costs and become more profitable. This may lead to more resources for expansions and higher stock prices.

Workers who control key know-how will be given incentives that are aligned with the business owners. In addition to salary and wages, they are likely to receive shares, stock options, or even cryptocurrencies as additional compensation. The division between a worker and a stakeholder through ownership and voting rights has become more blurred. The worker can be a shareholder in a publicly traded company or an architect of a new blockchain economy where rules and infrastructures are still being designed. They will need to develop the financial fluency to understand various instruments and become more invested in the business than ever.

SUMMARY OF INTRODUCTION

Disruptive technologies bring a myriad of rapid changes to our economic lives. They have an immediate impact on our career assumptions because jobs, or human tasks, will inevitably evolve to find better synergy with the more advanced machines we now operate. All jobs will need to adapt and evolve; some old jobs will become extinct while new ones emerge. The relationships we form around work will be different too. There is a lot more flexibility to organizing a productive work team, in terms of its size, geographical span, or workflow management. Workers will need to adopt new technologies to improve their individual productivity. In the future, the line between workers and business owners will become more blurred. Workers who have critical technological know-how will likely be granted more ownership of the business. As a result, they will need to form a view on the long-term prospects of the company they work for. They will also need to become more well versed in various means of investment because they are likely to encounter a more diverse set of financial incentives.

Technologies are rapidly shifting as new generations challenge and disrupt older ones. However, economics is a well-anchored science. Businesses and individual professionals all over the world are economically incentivized to maximize their utility and minimize their costs. Amid the crosscurrents of various disruptive technologies, we can adopt the principles of economics as an anchor to help us analyze their impact and formulate a strategy to preserve our own economic interests. With that, let's dive into the nineteen life-changing economic impacts of today's disruptive technologies. We'll start by quantifying AI's impact on jobs.

PART II

JOBS

Jobs give us the ability to make a living, to feed our families, and to sometimes even aim high and dream big. Jobs become part of our identity, as we spend a significant part of our lives training for them, doing them, and getting better at them.

This is why a common initial reaction to new technologies like AI is the fear of job loss. In 1960, John F. Kennedy, then a senator, announced that automation was "already threatening to destroy thousands of jobs and wipe out entire plants." This chapter will explore the impact of the latest technologies on our job market. How many jobs will they take? How will it impact the future of the workplace? Can they be helpful in any way?

CHAPTER **3**

GENERATIVE AI WILL DISRUPT 40% OF WORKING HOURS, BUT, NO, THERE WON'T BE MASS UNEMPLOYMENT

The blockbuster success of ChatGPT's commercial debut has been described as AI's iPhone moment. Various technologies supporting the smartphone had existed before, but the iPhone was the perfect sum of all these technologies packed into an intuitive design that fits right in the pocket. Since its launch, the iPhone has enabled a generation of new innovations that are centered around the smartphone's features and ecosystem. Similar to the iPhone, ChatGPT has brought easy-to-use, multifunctional, cutting-edge AI technology to the fingertips of average persons and businesses. Powerful AI technology existed before ChatGPT but was mostly reserved for tech specialists. Moreover, large language models like the one underlying ChatGPT can be further adapted for a wide range of tasks involving language skills. This means that businesses can leverage the very large pretrained models, finetune them according to their own business scenarios, and deploy them for specific job tasks. The customizability of the models is key to boosting the adoption rate of the technology because every business and every job have their own idiosyncratic features.

In 2023, Accenture, an IT consulting company, conducted a study to quantitatively assess the impact of generative AI on jobs. It studied over two hundred language-related job tasks found across various US industries and examined how AI may be adopted. Some of these tasks have a high potential for automation, where human involvement can be reduced and replaced by AI capacities. Many types of office and administrative support work fall into this category. Other tasks have a high potential for augmentation by AI, enabling human employees to be significantly more productive. For example, many software programming tasks fall into this category because machines can help human programmers write code more smoothly. However, human oversight remains important. The remaining tasks, such as construction and farming, have low potential for improvement from involving AI. The study concludes that 40% of all working hours across industries can be impacted by generative AI. Three industries with the highest share of working hours that can be either automated or augmented by AI are banking, insurance, and software.

Goldman Sachs, an investment bank, conducted a similar study on generative AI's job impact and suggested that three hundred million jobs around the world may be exposed to partial or full automation. Jobs in administrative support, legal, architecture, and engineering have the highest potential of being automated, whereas jobs that involve physical labor such as construction, installation, and cleaning are least at risk.

Will this lead to widespread joblessness? Economic history certainly suggests the answer is no. Since the mid-eighteenth century, which marked the beginning of the Industrial Revolution, unemployment rates across Western Europe and North America were mostly well below 10%. Three hundred years of technological development, including the invention of steam engines, automobiles, airplanes, mass-production techniques, computers, and the internet, was not enough to cause unemployment levels to rise above 10%. Only the Great Depression in the 1930s was able to push unemployment close to 20%. Macroeconomists believe the unemployment rate, the share of unemployed workers as a percentage of the total labor force, is primarily a result of short-term economic cycles. In other words, people are much more likely to lose their jobs because the economy is bad, not because science and technology are making big new strides.

The reason why technological breakthroughs are unlikely to lead to mass unemployment is that both jobs and workers are highly adaptable. For example, before electronic trading systems were available, buying and selling stocks used to involve retail investors making phone calls to their individual stockbrokers. Traders yelled at each other across the halls of stock exchanges to negotiate an execution price. Painless electronic stock trading has made such processes obsolete. You can now place a trading order on your smartphone. If your price is accepted by the market, within milliseconds, the trade will be executed. The great ease and convenience of the stock trading experience today has not led to massive unemployment and the downfall of the stock trading industry. In fact, it has enabled quite the opposite. Easy and hassle-free trading has encouraged more people to conduct stock trading activities, which creates a more active market where there are a lot of buyers and sellers at any given time. This is a highly attractive characteristic for many professional investors and traders who can then enter and exit their stock holdings easily—locking in profit or cutting loss as they see fit. More investment and trading activities create more jobs across the entire industry, including financial news, research, execution, legal, sales, and so on. Moreover, because the automated trading process comes at a lower cost to its provider, individual retail customers can enjoy low- or zero-commission trading, which saves them a lot of trading costs.

Nonetheless, it would be naïve to assume that new technology adoption will have little impact on the job market and the economic welfare of the working population. In the above example, the stock trading industry remains a large employer of salespeople, traders, and other professionals. But the job descriptions have changed, and the same talent who used to qualify for a top-paying job in the industry may no longer do so. The speed at which generative AI technology is being adopted is unprecedented. In this process, some workers will inevitably be displaced at least temporarily because new technology has taken their old jobs and they have yet to retrain or readjust to a new job.

Workers should stay alert to how their existing responsibilities can be disrupted or augmented by the latest technologies. The idea that one would spend years or even decades in training for a well-defined professional path may be an obsolete notion because new productive tools are available, and they are disrupting the way in which businesses are conducted. Individuals should learn to harness the power of new tools like generative AI, which, fortunately, are easy to use and require little knowledge of the underlying technology. Experienced industry professionals can offer tremendous value by finding ways to adapt these generic tools for the specific industry setting and to help overcome the inherent flaws in the AI models, such as hallucination, by providing human oversight and supervision. Employees who are earlier in their careers should stay open-minded about new opportunities, in and out of their current professions, that rise along with new technologies and tools. Overall workers

should proactively seize the opportunity to upgrade
their skills in conjunction with the new productive
AI tools and explore new possibilities in their professional careers. They should also draw the attention of
business leaders and policy makers to be mindful of
the social impact of radical changes in the job market.
More efforts should be directed at providing training
and reskilling to help match the demand of employers
with the supply of the right type of labor. The objective
is not just to reduce short-term unemployment but,
more importantly, to reduce skill mismatches or
underemployment.

CHAPTER **4**

THE MORE WE WORK WITH AI, THE MORE WE NEED HUMAN JUDGMENTS

AI can be used in a variety of applications, but its effectiveness varies greatly from one use case to another. In some cases, it can produce uncanny results that leave us in awe. The romantic poem that ChatGPT writes about quantum computing is funny and informative. It can put a little smile on the face of even a professional physicist. In other cases, however, AI may be little more than a counterproductive nuisance. Imagine putting ChatGPT in the consultation room as a specialist doctor with a patient who has a complicated and rare clinical condition. The AI chatbot may confidently spit out recommendations that sound like a professional diagnosis, but no doctors or patients would follow through with them.

AI requires two important preconditions to be effective for specific tasks. First, there should be a large amount of training information available for the task in question. Poems have been written for generations, and many papers have been published on the topic of quantum computing. There is a lot of training data for the AI to draw from when writing a poem about quantum computing. Meanwhile, medical records of patients are not readily available due to confidentiality constraints. For rare and complicated diseases, historical precedents may be very hard to come by. As such, the job of a specialist doctor relies heavily on the judgment of an experienced professional and is not solvable by a machine looking for a statistical resemblance with a large amount of past data. The more the AI has been trained on similar conditions, the better a chance it stands at making a high-quality prediction. Second, the stakes for if an AI makes a mistake should be acceptable. Hallucination is an inherent issue with AIs—which are based on statistical models, so they will always make mistakes. If an AI makes an erroneous statement about quantum computing in its romantic poem, this risk is manageable because it is unlikely to alter the course of modern physics. However, if an AI spits out an incorrect clinical diagnosis, it will affect the life of the patient. That is not a responsibility that an AI chatbot can or should take up. No sane authority would allow AI to have the power over such an important decision.

What kind of tasks are suitable for generative AI? Barak Turovsky, formerly a Google Language AI director, proposed that we evaluate each application in two categories: fluency and accuracy. Fluency describes how natural-looking and humanlike the AI results are. Tasks such as writing a poem, composing music, and writing reviews generally fall into this category. There, AI can produce content that feels like it has been written by another human being. Accuracy, meanwhile, describes how important it is for AI to produce the "right" answers rather than what "looks like" the right answers. For example, the diagnosis for the patient should be the right diagnosis rather than what "looks like" the right answer to untrained eyes. Generative AI tends to be very fluent because it has been trained on vast amounts of data from which it confidently extrapolates answers that look and feel like they may be human expert output. It tends not to be as good at being accurate because it is based on statistical models that look for the best fit with historical training data rather than understanding through a deterministic method that a certain answer definitely solves a certain question. This framework suggests that generative AI tools are more likely to be disruptive in areas that have a high fluency requirement but low accuracy requirement, such as the field of content creation. Meanwhile, for tasks that require high accuracy because the stakes are a lot higher, it is more likely that AI performs a supportive role to human professionals who are able to make better judgments.

Fundamentally, AI will continue to require human oversight in many tasks because AI cannot make judgments the same way humans do, despite its strong ability to make predictions. Predictions are based on finding the best statistical fit of the new input with training data. A prediction can be based on whether a new image shown is a cat or a dog, or what the next word in the sentence should be to make it sound more natural. On the other hand, judgment is the part of decision-making in which the various payoffs of different actions are evaluated against each other. In some cases, judgments are simple. An AI machine that is trained to play a board game has a clear objective: to win the game against its opponent while complying with the rules. Winning scores one and losing scores zero. However, most real-life situations require more complex judgment than that. In deciding what treatment to offer a patient with a complicated disease, for example, a specialist doctor will have to consider a wide range of sometimes conflicting factors, including the effectiveness of the treatment, its potential side effects, the impact on the patient's quality of life, and medical costs.

Human beings learn to make judgments from an early age. Sometime between eight and twelve months old, human babies start to understand the idea of "no" and will drop what they are doing when they are told no. Young children are taught that lying is bad and helping others is good. When we get older, we become capable of engaging in more complicated moral debates. Socrates, a Greek philosopher, suggested that one should not return a borrowed weapon to a friend who is not in his right mind, an example of two moral norms in conflict: repaying one's debts and protecting others from harm.

Without the right judgments, AI's ability to make good predictions can be problematic. The AI algorithms behind social media are powerful prediction machines. They maximize user stickiness by offering up content that is most likely to keep users active on the app. However, over a long period of time, these predictions may not be supportive of the collective social good. The excessive use of social media has hidden costs that include a lack of physical exercise and being more prone to mental health issues—especially for younger users. These are not factors that AI algorithms readily take into consideration.

Without human intervention, AI that has been trained on biased data may deepen existing biases without being instructed to do so. In 2018, Amazon stopped using an AI recruiting tool that showed a structural bias against women. Minority groups are likely to be underrepresented in the training data set to start with, and as a result, predictions for them are less accurate. This means machines can run the risk of more deeply entrenching existing inequality without intending to do so. AI may view women as less likely to be hired for a job which may deprive them of their fair share of employment opportunities and worsen gender inequality at work. Without human judgments and proactive efforts to rectify what is not right, AI can spread all kinds of societal biases.

Not all tasks are equally suited for AI. Regarding tasks that require a high level of accuracy or that have high stakes, AI is more likely to play a supportive role to humans. As AI enables faster, cheaper, and more predictions, there will be more need for human judgments. In these tasks, AI and human experts will be teaming up to enable better outcomes for the world by combining better predictions with better judgments.

CHAPTER **5**

SOME MANAGERIAL TASKS WILL BECOME OBSOLETE, BUT MANAGERS WON'T

Corporations are traditionally organized into hierarchies because it is more practical to group people into teams and manage them through layers of command. A 2006 study by the Wharton business school suggests that the ideal size of a working team is five people. A team this size can collectively solve the tasks at hand, but the team is still small enough that workflow communication is clear and individuals cannot "hide" their lack of contribution. Wharton's findings coincide with Amazon's "two-pizza rule," which was established by its founder and CEO, Jeff Bezos. The rule states that an effective meeting should be the size at which two pizzas could feed the whole group—or about five or six people. For a typical large corporation that employs a few thousand people, the entire workforce can be organized into about five or six layers of teams, each consisting of five or six members.

For individual workers, success in a career often means moving up the chain of command and becoming a manager. This professional evolution comes with a shift in the person's job responsibilities. Less time is spent performing specific job tasks, and more time is spent on managing. What exactly does managing entail? Some of the managerial responsibilities can be quite repetitive. These include allocating job tasks, monitoring project progress, reviewing work done by team members, and relaying information between the higher and lower levels of command. Other aspects of being a manager require creative input, a deep set of professional knowledge, and the charisma of a senior executive. These include motivating members of the team, hiring the best talent for the job, and putting them to work in areas that both fit the strategic priorities of the corporation and motivate them individually. Managers also often have to step out and address complicated issues when they are escalated by frontline workers, such as unusual customer complaints or difficult technical challenges.

There is significant room for an increased automation of routine managerial tasks. New technologies can and should replace the human hours spent on filling forms, updating information, and approving routine workflows. In 2020, Gartner, a research and consulting firm, predicted that 69% of a manager's routine workload will be fully automated by 2024. It also declared that 80% of project management tasks will be eliminated by 2030. AI, virtual reality, and digital platforms can monitor progress and collect and analyze data to improve overall performance outcomes. By reducing the repetitive tasks conducted by managers, technologies enable them to oversee larger teams more effectively, which would reduce the number of layers and the number of middle managers in the organization.

AI's success at conducting routine manager responsibilities has greatly empowered the gig economy. Gig workers are independent freelancers who are not bound by permanent employment contracts. They do not have predetermined working hours or preset annual performance targets. It would be very complicated for human managers to keep track of who is available at what hours, who the best-performing employees are, or how workers should be rewarded according to their performance. However, AI is perfectly suited to handle such tasks. Consider Uber, the popular ride-hailing app. There are approximately four million Uber drivers operating in more than ten thousand cities around the world. Not one has a direct manager. The app's interface gathers user requests, collects payments, monitors journeys in progress, and keeps track of user ratings. The real-time algorithm matches the nearest driver to a passenger and gives instant estimates on fare, wait time, and time of arrival. It also sends additional work toward better-performing drivers and deprioritizes or even fires poorly performing drivers. Critical routine functions usually performed by middle management have all been replaced by AI.

However, for more complicated professional tasks, AI is not yet ready to perform managerial roles on a large scale. The more specialized and complicated the tasks are, the more difficult it is for AI to judge how they should be allocated and how well they have been performed. While it is easy for Uber's AI manager to determine whether a driver has safely and speedily chauffeured the passenger to their destination, it is much more difficult to judge whether a doctor has performed their medical services well. The doctor can be judged by how friendly they are toward the patient, how thoroughly they explain the disease and the proposed treatment, the short-term effectiveness and the long-term side effects of the treatment, and the overall cost-effectiveness of their services. When boiled down to their essence, managerial tasks in complicated professional settings often require evaluating the various payoffs of different actions against each other. This type of task involves judgments, which, as we established earlier, are precisely the type of task that AI is not well equipped to do but humans excel at.

Instead of making managers obsolete, a wider adoption of AI can bring out the manager in individual professional workers. As AI takes up more repetitive and voluminous tasks, individual workers will encounter a shift in their job responsibilities similar to a promotion into the manager role. Skilled human workers are more likely to evaluate the recommen-dations made by AI and judge their pros and cons under various use cases or per different client preferences. They are more likely to intervene when an extraordinary circumstance arises that calls for a granular and customized solution. Microsoft 365 Copilot, the AI assistant feature for the company's widely used office software, will be able to take notes and create summaries of Teams meetings, convert text files into PowerPoint presentations, and set calendar invites according to the work plan. Historically, these professional tasks have been conducted by junior members of the professional team whose work progress is managed by more experienced professionals. With less time spent on routine tasks, we will have more time to evaluate, to strategize, and to be personal and creative. By performing more managerial roles, individual professional workers may feel a greater sense of pride and ownership in what they do, which may boost their productivity and workplace satisfaction.

CHAPTER **6**

SCALE UP
INDIVIDUAL SUCCESS
LIKE NEVER BEFORE

Today's AI, virtual reality, and digital platforms can make distant interactions feel close, large crowds feel more intimate, and mass-market recommendations feel more customized. This can broaden the reach of winning products and services because they can appeal to more customers in a more personal manner. Popular products and services can gain a larger following than before because they are less constrained by physical space and capacity limits.

Take the stunning rise of a sales megastar in China for example. A few years ago, Chinese e-commerce giant Alibaba started experimenting with livestream sales. A host would interact directly with an audience of potential buyers online. In 2018, a twenty-six-year-old cosmetics salesperson named Li Jiaqi gained a loyal following for the attention-grabbing way he sold lipstick. He would apply the lipstick and give instant reactions, which ranged from dramatic delight like "Oh my god, girls!" to scathing instructions to "Just trash it!" As a marketing gimmick, Li was even pitted against Alibaba founder Jack Ma, a celebrity in his own right, in a lipstick-selling contest. Unsurprisingly, Li won. Li subsequently replicated his lipstick success with numerous other products. His sales record grew exponentially over the next few years. At the biggest annual sales event of 2021, Li Jiaqi sold 10.6 billion Chinese yuan (equivalent to US$1.4 billion) worth of merchandise in one day. On that day, 249 million people watched his twelve-hour livestream event, and 35 million of those people walked away with a purchase.

Li's success as a salesperson is even more stunning when placed in the context of his physical competitors, brick-and-mortar malls in China. There are more than five thousand shopping malls in China. Only ten of these have ever reached annual sales values of more than 10 billion Chinese yuan (or US$1.4 billion), a record that Li broke in one day. The fact is, most malls are finding it difficult to compete with the online shopping experience, where recommendations are more tailored, prices more competitive, and choices more abundant.

In economics, "winner takes all" describes the situation where a product or service provider is favored over its competitors and the provider is able to capture substantially all of the market share and economic profit. Besides a better product or service offering (even if only slightly), there are a few preconditions for "winner takes all." First, the marginal cost should be very low. This is often the case with digitally enabled products and services. There is virtually no difference in cost, whether Li's livestream sales event is transmitted to one customer or two hundred million potential buyers at the same time. Second, there is no capacity limit. While a salesperson working from a department store counter does not have the space to handle more than a handful of customers, it is free and unlimited seating for all in an online sales show. Finally, the network effect and platform effect kick in. Users love to congregate where other users are because it enables them to be part of a broader community—this is the network effect. They also enjoy the convenience of sourcing multiple goods and services from one provider, once they establish trust—this is the platform effect. Together, these factors create a virtuous cycle for the winning services provider. As soon as the provider identifies a unique stronghold in a niche, which in Li's case was his uncanny ability to sell lipsticks, it can quickly scale up its offerings and improve its economics while doing so. As it scales up, the cost of providing the services remains largely constant, but the services become more competitive against its competitors and more appealing to its customers. The winner ends up taking a substantial part of the overall market share.

A range of disruptive technologies enabled Li's success.

To start with, AI algorithms drive product recommendations, backed by a large amount of data. While individual tastes vary, brands and products with a proven track record tend to stand a better chance of becoming the next hit. Beyond choosing from the bestseller chart, the recommendation algorithm also digs into a lot more granularity. A new brand may be rapidly gaining a cult following among customers with a certain demographic profile, such as students with a tight budget who are looking for classroom-friendly make-up. Another product may be uniquely suitable for a previously underserved use case, such as ultralong wear in very humid weather. AI is particularly good at identifying small but persistent patterns in data that can predict the long-term success of a product. The better the recommendation system, the more likely customers are going to walk away with a pleasant purchase and the more likely they are to return to the same salesperson.

Second, the online lipstick sales experience was supported by augmented reality tools. Alibaba's shopping app allows users to try on different cosmetic products using their phone's camera. It is like looking at yourself in a mirror, with the cosmetic product you are considering buying digitally added to your face. Shoppers can see how the color fits with their skin tones and how the texture applies to the skin type. At the swipe of your fingers, the digital make-up may be swapped for an alternative look with a different set of products on sale.

Finally, the network effect really stands out in a virtual space. Because the digital experience can be infinitely scaled up, it can enable a strong sense of community among its many customers. Li Jiaqi is a charming screen personality with an approachable and authentic aura. He developed a connection with his viewers that resembled the relationship between a celebrity and his fans more than a salesman and his customers. Regulars at his virtual shop supported him through his various business and entertainment endeavors. They also connected among themselves and take pride in their shared identity, who the sales star fondly refers to as "all my young ladies."

Disruptive technologies enabled and amplified the phenomenal success of this sales megastar. The new data-driven augmented-reality-supported sales approach on a large digital platform replaced the traditional way. For generations, lipstick has been sold over beauty counters in department stores, which involves a customer physically trying on the product while a salesperson painstakingly makes a pitch. Once the new sales method gained traction, it rapidly scaled up into a full-blown victory against other competitors and brick-and-mortar malls because the economies of scale are very compelling in a digitally enabled business. Before his ascent to stardom, Li Jiaqi briefly worked as a beauty salesperson in an unremarkable brick-and-mortar shopping mall where he first learned his craft. His sweeping success is the result of a combination of luck, grit, and disruptive technologies that can support the extraordinary success of a talent at an unprecedented scale.

CHAPTER **7**

SUSTAIN OUR PASSION, REDUCE BURNOUT, SOLVE IMPORTANT PROBLEMS, AND BE MORE CREATIVE IN OUR JOBS

New technologies can help human talents focus on the more interesting aspects of their jobs, feel more empowered, and stay more motivated about their professional passion. This can improve the longevity of careers and ultimately help our society benefit from the more meaningful work done by our talented individuals. This can also help individuals prevent burnout and accomplish more professionally.

Burnout is an occupational syndrome classified by the World Health Organization. It describes the situation where a worker experiences depletion of energy, increased mental distance from their job, and reduced professional efficacy. While burnout is not a clinical diagnosis, some experts believe other conditions such as depression are behind it. Burnout is a widespread occupational hazard. A survey performed by Deloitte, an auditing and consulting company, revealed that 77% of full-time workers across different sectors of the United States have experienced burnout in their current job. Top reasons for burnout include unrealistic deadlines or expectations and consistently long working hours. Interestingly, passion for a job does not prevent workplace burnout; 87% of the people in the same survey said they are still passionate about their current jobs—they are just mentally exhausted.

The COVID-19 pandemic has further exacerbated burnout issues, especially among healthcare professionals. A 2021 survey led by the American Medical Association found that 63% of US physicians experienced burnout in 2021, compared with 38% in 2020. Another survey in 2022 found that one in five physicians say they will likely leave their current practice within two years. In the United States, it costs more than US$1 million to train a physician and nearly double that amount to train a surgeon. The minimum time it takes to train a doctor is over a decade, including time spent in relevant undergraduate studies, medical school, and medical residency. An experienced specialist practitioner takes multiple decades. Reducing burnout and making a career in healthcare more sustainable benefits both the collective public good by saving costs and professional individuals by helping them go further in their professional progression.

AI has shown promise in assisting many areas of the healthcare profession. Natural language processing, for example, can assist with the clinical documentation of patient records and medical research indexing. Medical triage, the practice of assigning different priorities of treatment based on how acute the medical needs are, can be made more effective and automated. Surgical robots can help surgeons conduct precise and minimally invasive operations. Wearable sensors and health monitors reduce the workload of routine patient data collection at the hospital. This frees up medical resources to be devoted to better serving more complex patient cases. AI is effective at reducing human burnout due to the simple fact that it does not get tired and does not have a complicated motivational system. By quietly churning away, machines can help us sift through voluminous tasks and focus on the ones that are most challenging, idiosyncratic, and require the most professional judgment.

In some instances, AI is not just able to alleviate the workload of human professionals but also improve their effectiveness. Among the most promising applications of AI in healthcare is diagnostic imaging in the clinical field, where AI assists radiologists. Radiologists typically spend long hours in front of computer screens processing large quantities of similar images. Not surprisingly, they experience a particularly high rate of burnout. Computer-aided diagnostics have shown excellent accuracy and sensitivity for the detection of radiographic abnormalities. In 2018, a group of MIT researchers reportedly found a machine-learning algorithm that can process 3D brain scans a thousand times more quickly than when done manually. Machines can also identify abnormalities early, when they are much smaller—even too small for the human eye to see. While human radiologists still need to make a prognosis and assess any uncommon conditions, by incorporating more AI assistance, diseases can be better prevented and treated earlier, and at a lower cost to both the public health system and the patients.

In addition to reducing burnout, new technologies can also help us move faster when trying to solve really important problems such as curing cancer.

In 2022, shockwaves went through the biological science community when AlphaFold, an AI model, predicted the structures of every known protein on the planet. This conclusively solved "the folding problem" that human biologists have spent decades working on. In the natural world, amino acids—small organic compounds that are the basic building blocks of life—join together to form chains. These chains then spontaneously fold into native structures to form proteins. These uniquely folded 3D structures are what give proteins their wide range of functions, like brain activity, muscle building, insulin regulation, and antibodies that fight disease. The reason "the folding problem" is so complex is because a typical protein with a length of about three hundred amino acids could theoretically make more than 10^{390} different 3D structures. This is such an enormous number that to produce just one molecule of each kind would require many more atoms than exist in the universe.

Prior to AI models making effective predictions, protein structures could only be determined experimentally by a few expensive and time-consuming techniques performed in biology labs. Since the 1960s, laboratory efforts have determined the 3D structure of about 170,000 proteins, or less than 0.1% of over two hundred million known natural proteins. The AlphaFold model was trained on the structure information of these known proteins to predict the vast number of unknown structures with astounding accuracy. In 2021, the AlphaFold methodology was published as a paper in *Nature*, a leading science journal, alongside open-source software. In 2022, the 3D structures of all two hundred million proteins were uploaded into the AlphaFold Protein Structure Database, free of charge, available for anyone to use.

Decoding the full set of protein structures has significant implications for medical and biological science. Understanding the 3D structure of proteins in mutated cancer cells, for example, can help us identify the type of drugs that can bind to the surface of these problematic proteins and inhibit their growth. In other words, thanks to the contribution made by the AI model, we are now one big step closer to curing cancer.

In addition to their practical uses, new technologies

can also enable us to be more creative. Throughout history, artists have been pushing the boundaries on what constitutes art by adopting an ever wider set of tools and challenging artistic notions. The media of creation have evolved from single-medium work, such as oil painting on canvas, to mixed media, which includes paint, cloth, and wood; from permanent objects, such as bronze statues, to transient spectaculars, such as artists who paint with explosives; and from physical objects, such as a painting or a sculpture, to digital, such as NFTs stored on a blockchain. The source of artistic inspiration has also evolved. Artists from medieval times expressed stories from the Bible almost exclusively, which is a narrow set of themes to draw inspiration from. The renaissance saw artists shifting focus onto the everyday lives of ordinary people. This opens up whole new dimensions of stories to be told and observations to be made. New technologies allow us to draw from a larger set of inputs than ever and produce art in forms that have never existed before.

Refik Anadol, a Turkish-American artist, is known for using machine-learning algorithms to create new media artworks. In one of his installations in the Museum of Modern Art (MoMA) in New York City, called *Unsupervised*, he trained an AI model to interpret the MoMA's collection of 130,000 works spanning over two hundred years of modern art history. As the model "walks" through the collection, it digests the history of modern art, incorporates the live environment of the museum on a given day, and provides its live output. The digital artwork is displayed on a 24 x 24 ft screen that unfolds in real time, continuously generating otherworldly shapes and forms that engulf viewers in a large-scale abstract installation. The result is a continuously shifting feast of dreamlike imagery and sound.

Anadol aptly describes his works as machine's dreams and hallucinations. In AI terminology, hallucination is when machines produce results that look and feel like the correct answers but are, in fact, false. In practical settings, hallucination is often a problem because it undermines the accuracy of AI's predictions and its usability in many scenarios where finding the one true answer is important. However, the art world is precisely where the boundaries of truth and untruth, dream and reality, past and future, are intentionally blurred to provoke thoughts regarding these established concepts. Anadol's art challenges the common perception of AI as analytical, quantitative, and unromantic and explores its capability for fantasy and sentimentality.

AI can enable people to work in a meaningful way. Individuals can avoid burnout, focus on the part of their responsibilities that are challenging and exciting, preserve career longevity, be equipped with more resources to support their work, and be more creative on a massive scale. Societally, it helps us gainfully retain our best human talent in a sustainable manner, make big strides in solving important issues, and push creative boundaries in a way we have never imagined before.

CHAPTER **8**

EXPERIMENT WITH
BOLD IDEAS
CONSEQUENCE-FREE

The powerful combination of AI, VR, and other recent technologies can create high-quality digital twins of real-world environments, such as an office, a factory, a train station, or a warehouse. These digital twins are photorealistic copies of the physical world that allow us to participate from various perspectives. We can have a bird's-eye view of the train station or go immersively to the platform as virtual passengers. The digital twins abide by the same laws of physics and movement patterns of the real world. The trajectory of an object will be subject to the same forces of gravity, friction, airflow, and the like. Passengers will move about the station, exhibiting the same behavioral patterns as they would in the real world. The availability of these digital twins has a huge impact on how business decisions will be made.

To understand their economic significance, we need to first revisit the concept of rationality. The study of economics assumes that we are all rational beings who are always incentivized to maximize our utility. When faced with several options, we should always choose the one that represents the most utility for us. In many cases, the economic outcomes are uncertain. An investment can generate a positive return or a loss. A business partner may prove worthy or unreliable. When faced with such uncertainty, we will incorporate the probability of each scenario into our consideration—our expected utility would be the probability-weighted average of utilities across the various scenarios. For example, suppose someone offers to flip a coin. We will win one dollar if the coin lands on heads and lose one if the coin lands on tails. We should feel indifferent about playing this game because the probability-weighted return of this game is zero. Now imagine this person offers to change the payout of the game. We will win the same amount if the coin lands on heads, but no money changes hands if the coin lands on tails. In other words, heads we win, tails we don't lose. This alters our probability-weighted expected utility from zero to $0.50 (calculated as $1*50%+0*50%). As a result, we should rationally choose to play the game because our expected return is now positive instead of neutral. In this case, the positive utility from an upside scenario remains intact while the negative utility from a downside scenario has been eliminated, and the probability distribution of the utility outcome is now skewed toward potential gain. We are economically incentivized to take the risk.

Preserving the upside and eliminating the downside is exactly the economic incentive at play when digital twins are created to solve real-world issues because they allow us to experiment consequence-free. The digital twin can allow us to study the current status quo and incorporate proposed changes for an intended physical environment. This allows us to interact with various components, using real-world physics and behavioral habits to make modifications and test out ideas. If an incremental change proves helpful to the overall process, then it can be implemented in the real world. If the incremental change does not pan out positively, it can be painlessly undone in the digital format. This is particularly helpful when there are large numbers of complex variables at play in determining the outcome of our experiments.

In May 2022, BMW, a German automaker, announced the company will create digital twins for all their existing and future factories. The objective is to be more "flexible, efficient, sustainable, and digital." The ability to visualize and stress test major investments before putting them into physical practice can save lots of time, reduce carbon footprints, and avoid costly mistakes. This allows the company to implement both extensive new planning and small-scale ongoing finetuning in an efficient and flexible manner. Full digitalization of the plants will also improve the data consistency across the company and its business partners. The automotive industry operates on a notoriously complex supply chain. Improving data quality across the external supply chain and internal process chains can provide more clarity for decision-making across the ecosystem.

Today's technologies allow us to create not just one digital twin but as many parallel universes as we want. This can allow us to iterate virtual experiments as many times as we need and greatly accelerate the speed at which new ideas are tested for real-world implementation. For example, take the training of driverless cars in real traffic. Autonomous vehicles need to be trained in complicated traffic conditions in order to drive well in them, but their training can disrupt busy traffic and put real lives in danger—this is a classic chicken and egg problem. In 2023, San Francisco allowed empty autonomous vehicles to drive on local roads during the daytime. This was met with local complaints about driverless cars idling in the middle of the roads, causing traffic jams, and disrupting emergency services. Other cities around the world may become more reluctant than the tech-friendly neighbor of Silicon Valley to allow real-world testing of autonomous vehicles on their local roads, which can slow down the localized training of such technologies. One way to address regulators' concerns would be to create a large number of digital replicas of the world's busiest cities and train autonomous vehicles in them. The more this technology has been trained in realistic traffic via large-scale simulations, the less likely they are to pose issues when they actually reach the roads.

Consequence-free digital experimentation and large-scale simulation allow us to be bolder and take more risks in our professional decision-making. More ideas are likely to leave the whiteboard in a team discussion room or an employee's head and be tested out at minimal cost in the digital parallel universe. When the cost of experimentation is high, only the ideas that are most likely to succeed are put through actual tests. These could be ideas put forward by the most senior person in the team or ideas that "feel" the safest, which typically comply with established practices. Professional decision-making is less likely to take a leap of faith, whether in new employees or in outrageous ideas. However, when the cost of experimentation is dramatically lowered, more ideas can be tested out more easily. We are likely to be more innovative, think more outside the box, and be more meritocratically judged. This can foster a more dynamic working environment where we are rewarded for taking more risks and being bold.

PART III

INCOME AND PROFIT

Disruptive technologies will impact our collective economic life by changing how much we produce and how much we consume. Labor and capital go into the productive process as the two sources of input. Goods and services come out of the productive process as outputs that are then sold to generate revenue. As a reward for the productive process, labor earns wages and salaries as income, while capital receives profit. In other words, the economic output of any productive process is distributed between income for labor and profit for capital.

The following chapter studies how disruptive technologies impact the total economic output and its distribution. Different individuals, corporations, and regions will have different shares of the overall economic pie, which will lead to different economic fates.

CHAPTER **9**

THE TOTAL ECONOMIC PIE GROWS, A LOT

In a report called "Size the Prize," PwC, an auditing and consulting company, quantifies how AI can add to the world's total economic output. It estimates that world GDP may be up to 14% higher in 2030 thanks to AI contribution. On an annual basis, AI's incremental boost to GDP growth is equivalent to up to 1.5% per year. Given that world GDP growth has averaged about 3% per year over the past decades, this means AI technologies alone can accelerate the pace of world economic growth rate by half in the next decade or so.

Researchers at PwC quantified the economic impact of AI by conducting both bottom-up studies and top-down economic analyses. In the bottom-up part of the study, AI impact was measured for its ability to enhance quality and consistency, save time, and provide more customizations for different application scenarios in different industries. The top-down process looked at how AI can make us more productive and create new products and jobs while disrupting old ones around the world. The report found that the bulk of the initial impact of AI was a productivity boost, including the automation and augmentation of current procedures, from voluminous routine responsibilities to high-impact tasks. The bulk of the economic impact then shifts to an increase in consumer demand. The productivity boost offered by AI is likely to improve the quality and the customization of products and services offered, which makes them more likely to appeal to us. The possible work hours freed by AI may also allow us more time for "play." This can also increase our consumption.

Researchers also suggest that the economic gains from AI will be uneven across regions. Two regions that are likely to benefit the most from AI are China and North America, where the boost to GDP in 2030 is estimated to be 26% and 14% respectively. North America is expected to realize its AI benefits faster because it is currently ahead in terms of research and technology. Meanwhile, China will likely adopt AI technology more slowly because it will need more time to build the necessary expertise. Nonetheless, China has a higher portion of GDP that comes from industrial activities, where the productivity gain from introducing AI technologies may be greater and more scalable. In around ten years' time, China's productivity will begin to pull ahead of the global stage.

It is not surprising that China and North America stand to benefit the most from the next generation of AI technologies. These two regions already represent the world's largest economies. They are also home to the world's most successful tech companies, from Apple and Amazon to Tencent, the creator of the world's super app WeChat, and ByteDance, the company behind TikTok. Developing and implementing new technologies often requires a whole innovative value chain, including academic resources, business environments, regulatory frameworks, capital market funding, and talent retention programs. Places that already have these infrastructures are likely to experience continued success in implementing the next generation of new technologies.

CHAPTER **10**

BIG TECHS GET MUCH BIGGER IN AN UNLEVELED PLAYING FIELD

Building today's disruptive technologies requires significant investments in both software and hardware. This can lead to an uneven playing field where companies that have deep financial resources or are connected to such resources are more likely to succeed.

The popular chatbot ChatGPT is built on the foundational model GPT-4. Foundational models are AI models trained on broad data so that they can perform a wide range of tasks. Training these foundational models is expensive because it requires very significant computing power. GPT-4 is part of the GPT series of foundational models created by OpenAI. It was released in March 2023, merely one year after its predecessor GPT-3.5. GPT-4 cost more than US$100 million to train. The next generation of GPT model, GPT-5, is expected to be bigger and cost even more to train. Not only is training the models expensive, but operating them is also very costly. According to SemiAnalysis, a research company, ChatGPT costs OpenAI as much as US$700,000 per day to operate in 2023. The cost of operation is expected to eventually normalize to a much more affordable level as the cost of computing power comes down gradually. But before that, the model remains an expensive endeavor. To fund these expensive investments and operating costs, OpenAI has raised a total of US$11.3 billion in funding from its various investors, including tech giants like Microsoft.

Meta has also funded its ambition for a dominant position in the VR and AR business with heavy investments. The company makes a loss of over US$10 billion each year in Reality Lab, the division that has been responsible for its AR, VR, and immersive technologies. It is unclear whether this line of business will become profitable in the near future, and some investors think this can be a decade-long, US$100 billion initiative for the company. Only a handful of companies or even governments in this world can afford investments this size. In comparison, the 2022 US federal government's total spending on infrastructure was US$36 billion, which covers everything from roads and power lines to water storage facilities across the country.

As cutting-edge technologies rapidly develop, incumbent leaders try to stay ahead of their competition by reinvesting aggressively to widen their technological lead. In some cases, the industry's leader is so well ahead of everyone else that it becomes an effective monopoly.

Taiwan Semiconductor Manufacturing Company Limited (TSMC) is the world's leading semicon-ductor manufacturer. Modern semiconductor chips control everything from smartphones to life support machines. While the raw material, silicon, is abundantly available, the technology needed to turn silicon into semiconductor chips is very complex.

Semiconductor chips are manufactured in foundries, where tiny electronic circuits are drawn on silicon wafers through a series of highly specialized steps. These steps require a high level of precision and utilize equipment that can cost more than 300 million USD apiece. As a result, foundries are expensive to build. In December 2022, TSMC announced its latest foundry in Arizona will cost US$40 billion.

The rapid evolution of the semiconductor industry creates a self-reinforcing cycle of competitor advantage for the incumbent leader in the industry. The chip's iteration is governed by Moore's law, which states that the processing power of a chip would double every eighteen months to two years. iPhones today have more than one hundred thousand times the processing power of the computer that first landed a man on the moon fifty years ago. Under the rapid iteration of technology, there is consistent demand for products built with the latest technological features, which can lead to strong pricing power for these manufacturers. Higher pricing power leads to high profits, which can allow the company to invest in ways that ensure it will be the first to provide the next level of technology. Meanwhile, competitors who cannot manufacture the most advanced chips can only charge a moderate price from customers, earning a small profit, and would not be able to afford to invest in the next generation of manufacturing technology.

An effective monopoly is established when lagging competitors simply cannot afford to catch up. Indeed, the history of chip manufacturing reveals a thinning field of players. Twenty years ago, the most advanced chips were manufactured by more than a dozen producers across the United States, Japan, Taiwan, and Europe. In 2018, only three companies were able to produce the most advanced chips. These are TSMC of Taiwan, Samsung of Korea, and Intel of the United States. As of 2023, only TSMC is expected to be able to commercially produce the next generation of chips.

The technology industry longs for monopolistic power similar to what TSMC commands. Peter Thiel, an entrepreneur and venture capitalist, declared to his fellow entrepreneurs, "Competition is for losers. Build a monopoly!" There is an ongoing rush by tech giants to build the infrastructure that would support the next generation of disruptive technology. By making heavy up-front investments that only a handful of companies in the world can afford to make, they are betting that they can establish a strong lead over other players in the field, attract a wide user base, generate a generous recurring income, and reinforce their leadership position in the field.

Big corporations are likely to become even bigger and more powerful in the latest technological race. They command more financial resources to start with, so they can invest heavily in the newest technology, which can sometimes be experimental and risky in nature. Over time, they are more likely to debut products that are well ahead of their competitors and command bargaining power over their customers, suppliers, and even employees who would congregate where other talents and resources are. This makes it more difficult for smaller competitors or new entrepreneurs to compete in the field. Given heavy up-front investments, low marginal cost of ongoing operation, and a potentially self-reinforcing barrier to entry, their products and services can become so pervasive in our everyday lives. It is therefore imperative for the general public and regulators to remain watchful of the corporate powers of the technology industry to ensure that they remain constructive, rather than destructive, to the rest of society.

CHAPTER **11**

OUR RELATIONSHIPS WITH THE BIG TECHS BECOME MORE COMPLICATED

The major tech companies are so pervasive in our lives that we develop multifaceted economic relationships with them. We can be their paying customers, loyal users, and followers of their arbitrary rules. We may be employed directly by them, or our jobs may be indirectly linked to the extensive ecosystem that revolves around the technology sector. We are often investors in these companies through direct investment, funds, or retirement savings. Our economic interests are deeply intertwined with those of these industry titans.

Apple is a classic example of a large company that has inspired strong loyalty and forged a deep connection with its users. Apple's core business is selling electronic products, such as MacBooks, iPhones, iPads, and Apple Watches, and its customers are often recurring buyers of these products. A survey by CIRP, a consumer research firm, found that over 60% of Apple users own three to four devices from the company. Apple users tend to be wealthier individuals who value security, privacy, and the smooth operating experience of one of the world's most premium smartphones. They are often willing to pay an extra price for the product and services, regardless of short-term economic fluctuation. Even in the challenging market conditions of 2022, when the world faced the lingering effects of the COVID-19 pandemic and consumer confidence was weak, the iPhone managed to gain smartphone market share at the expense of almost every other major competitor in the world, despite being more expensive.

Big, powerful corporations can make us follow their rules without question. Some of these rules can be so arbitrary that they go against conventional wisdom and defy common sense. Apple continues to be a good example. Apple's App Store is the marketplace where users can download apps developed for the Apple ecosystem, mostly by third parties. Apple charges a 30% commission on all apps and in-app purchases, as well as first-year subscription fees. In other words, if you paid US$10 to purchase a game created by a third-party developer, US$7 goes to the people who have painstakingly built the game, while US$3 goes to Apple as commission and adds to the company's colossal profit stream of nearly US$100 billion a year. Is 30% a "normal" commission level to charge its users? Probably not. An average real estate agent in the United States charges 5% of the final property price as commission. Many stockbrokers offer zero commissions for stock trading services, and those who do charge a fee usually take a cut well below 1% of the transaction value. Apple's App Store commission revenue is so high compared to the cost of maintaining the service that it is estimated that this line of business generates a profit margin of nearly 80%. How did Apple come up with their 30% commission rate? It was a legacy feature inherited from the iTunes store, where the company used to sell digital music to its users. Building on the phenomenal success of the iPod in the late 1990s and early 2000s, Steve Jobs announced that all songs on iTunes could be downloaded legally for ninety-nine cents each, of which only sixty-five cents went to the music label. At the time, music labels were struggling with rampant music piracy but did not have the capability to distribute music electronically, which was increasingly the customer preference. This created a space for Apple to make an extraordinary rule that still holds today.

Big tech companies are important job creators. The tech sector is a major employer of workers, and through their ecosystem of partners and suppliers, they create a large number of jobs, often relatively well paid, all over the world. In the United States, the tech industry accounts for $1.9 trillion, or more than 10% of the country's GDP. It provides 12.1 million jobs, which represents 8% of the country's total jobs outstanding. Within local communities, tech jobs, which are on average better paid compared to other jobs, are often a boost to the economy. The lives and the jobs of the tech workers and their families can in turn support many other businesses and jobs, which include restaurants, shops, clinics, and other services. Across the supply chain, tech-related employment opportunities come in all forms from around the world. Apple directly employs eighty thousand people and estimates that it creates a total of two million jobs in the United States alone. Outside its home country, Apple works with more than 180 suppliers in more than fifty countries, and millions of workers around the world find employment on its supply chain.

The tech sector also affects our financial well-being because many of us have a meaningful share of our personal wealth invested in them, either directly or indirectly, knowingly or unknowingly. The average American household holds equity as their largest form of wealth storage, which ranks ahead of their homes. As of the first quarter of 2023, US households have an aggregate net worth of US$148 trillion, of which US$42 trillion is invested in equities and US$41 trillion is invested in real estate. Big tech companies form a very large share of the overall stock market. Apple, Microsoft, Amazon, Nvidia, and Alphabet are the top five constituents of the S&P 500, a commonly adopted stock index in the United States. Collectively, these five companies account for 24% of the index and dominate its performance. The total exposure of US households to these five tech companies is equivalent to five to six months of the aggregate income of these households. The more profit these large tech companies reap, and the more speedily they do it, the higher their stock prices will be, and the more our personal wealth appreciates accordingly.

Each of these large tech companies plays a pivotal role in enabling the latest disruptive technologies. Nvidia is a company that specializes in making graphic processing units, or GPUs. GPUs are used in a variety of tasks, including training advanced AI models, making immersive digital 3D spaces come to life through visual graphics, and conducting blockchain activities. Microsoft is a large shareholder of OpenAI, the company behind the sweeping success of ChatGPT. Microsoft is also expected to launch the Copilot function in its Office 365 software, which will allow AI capabilities to be easily adopted into office tools. Apple has recently announced Apple Vision Pro, a mixed reality headset that the company describes as its first spatial computer. Amazon, through its Amazon Web Services subsidiary, is a main provider of cloud computing services. The demand for their services is expected to rise significantly as more computing is expected to be done over the cloud; massive amounts of digital information will need to be stored, processed, transmitted, and computed through the cloud infrastructure. Finally, Alphabet, the holding company of Google, is home to one of the largest pools of AI experts in the industry. It has built the theoretical framework that underlies today's generative AIs.

Our complicated relationship with the big tech corporations is fundamentally because they have gained so much economic power and pervaded so many aspects of our lives. This has created many touch points between us and intertwined our economic interests. We depend on them for essential digital services and are often at their mercy regarding fees and terms of service. They may represent coveted workplaces that offer opportunities to fulfill our career ambitions and earn a handsome salary. They also represent a substantial share of our financial investments and personal wealth. The long-term success of these corporations can affect the quality of our retirement lives.

This intricate mesh of sometimes conflicting economic interests at play makes it difficult to judge whether it is to our benefit that these big technology companies are likely to control and build many of the disruptive technologies today. We should instead take a more granular approach when forming our opinions of these companies. Just because a substantial share of personal wealth may be tied to the stock performance of these companies does not mean we should tolerate abusive market behaviors that unfairly stifle competition from smaller players. As these companies become bigger and more complex for the general public or regulators to form a conclusive opinion on, it is important that society still continues to evaluate them based on the same principles of corporate governance and social responsibilities that we would apply to any company, regardless of size.

CHAPTER **12**

THE INVISIBLE HAND MAY CREATE "TWO AMERICAS"

The success of the big tech companies is not an issue in itself, but a widening gap between the prosperous big tech companies and the rest of the economy, whose growth potential may be significantly lower, can be problematic. Such dichotomy may prevent economic policies from functioning properly and prevent real people and businesses from receiving the support that is intended for them, leading to an unbalanced playing field, where some areas of the economy are structurally underinvested. This can also lead to asset bubbles in the market as capital blindly pours into a select few investment destinations without considering the consequences. It may even lead to severe market turbulence and deep investor losses that take years to repair.

The success of the big tech companies is often built on a core set of disruptive technologies, which can power a sustained period of extraordinary growth. When disruptive technologies find the right applications in real-life business scenarios, they can create brand-new business models that break down the old playbook of traditional industries. This happened with search engines and social networks two decades ago, and it can happen again with AI and VR technologies today. Just like how Google used its powerful search engines to disrupt online advertising and become one of the largest advertisers in the world, AI and VR technologies can be highly adaptable and change the way products are displayed, services are customized, and people are connected. When disruptive technologies find the appropriate use cases, they can structurally take market share from the incumbent players over a sustained period of time. A company that grows at 15% per year, a common growth rate for big tech companies, will be more than three times bigger in ten years' time compared to an incumbent player, which grows at 2%–3%, the long-term average of US GDP growth rate. Investors love such compounding growth stories and will offer their stamps of approval to these business models by buying stock in them, even at hefty valuations.

Over time, these big tech stocks become such attractive investments that capital and resources keep pouring in. The market can remain exuberant about the extraordinary growth opportunities of this small group of companies, which represent a dispropor-tionately large share of the stock market. In doing so, the market may neglect how the rest of the economy is doing—even if the rest of the economy is in a fragile state and policy makers are battling stubborn issues such as sticky inflation and banking crises. During the first six months of 2023, the S&P index has gone up 16%, a handsome gain for stock market investors. However, the picture is a lot less rosy if one looks elsewhere in the economy. The Small Business Optimism Index, a monthly sentiment gauge of small businesses in the US, slumped to its weakest in more than a decade in May 2023. Three midsize banks have gone bust within the year 2023. Average households have been dealing with escalating living expenses amid decades-high inflation.

The disconnect between the excellent performance of a very small group of big tech companies and the vast majority of the economy threatens the effectiveness of public economic policies. The capitalist economy is moved by the "invisible hand," an apt metaphor by eighteenth-century philosopher and economist Adam Smith, which states that capital resources are drawn to where the most abundant rewards are expected to be. The government, in principle, will not tell corporations what to produce or how much. Instead, policy makers such as the Federal Reserve, or the Fed, adjust macroeconomic policies based on the prevailing economic conditions. When the economy is weak, the Fed will lower interest rates and make it easier for corporations to access capital by making money more abundant. The issue with a crowded big tech space is that a disproportionally large share of the incremental monetary stimulus will always end up, through free market forces, with their already lofty stock prices. Small businesses and the vast majority of the rest of the economy may not be able to receive the capital they need to restore growth and confidence. The prosperity of a small group of elite companies masks the vulnerability of the economic condition of a much wider group of people. The lack of funding and investments can further discourage innovation, which makes them even more likely to be disrupted by powerful, cash-rich corporations.

If such conditions persist, we may face the problem of "Two Americas," or a clear division of the economic potential in any major economy between the haves and the have-nots due to a dysfunctional allocation of resources. The haves are the big tech companies. They can afford to attract the brightest talent and offer them the most competitive compensation and career prospects. The have-nots are all the other businesses that may be smaller in scale, promise fewer growth opportunities, and draw less interest from investors and policymakers. The 2011 science fiction novel *Ready Player One* paints a dystopian picture of what that may be like in an extreme scenario. In this imaginary land, people seek to escape from the ramshackle physical world into a lustrous virtual reality world. Reality represents the old world, which people have largely abandoned in favor of the new world. Things were falling apart, and no one really cared. The virtual world is a space controlled by a powerful technology company that provides all types of entertainment, excitement, hopes, and pleasures for people. Society seems to only care about what happens in the new and lustrous space of the virtual reality world. Over time, the gap between the crumbly old world and the shining new world becomes bigger.

What can we do to prevent our world from drifting apart like this? To start with, we should say no to the monopolistic behaviors of individual companies. For example, individual users can reject abusive market behavior such as the forced collection of individual data. Second, we should keep our eyes open to all available options of products and service providers, including large corporations, small businesses, or nonprofit and open-source solutions. We should also support public policies that offer targeted support to people or businesses in need and be mindful of the social impact of our economic decisions. Finally, when we invest our personal savings, we should beware of the risk of the market chasing a narrow set of companies to unreasonably high stock prices. The dot-com bubble in the late 1990s was accompanied by a period of genuine technological innovation. At the time, new technologies such as the internet showed seemingly limitless potential to change the world, and eager investors were ready to chase the stocks of internet companies at whatever cost. Between 1995 and 2000, the NASDAQ, a tech-focused stock index, went up 800%. However, the valuation of these tech companies became so stretched that the NASDAQ eventually collapsed in 2000, wiping out nearly 80% of its peak valuation. It took the index fifteen years to cross the height of the dot-com bubble again in 2015. In other words, if an investor had entered the market at its peak to save for their children's education, by the time they recovered their initial investments at face value, their children would have already graduated high school.

CHAPTER **13**

THE MIDDLE CLASS WILL
NEED THE MOST HELP

Income inequality is an old social issue. In the United States, the rich have been getting richer for the past few decades. Data from the US Census Bureau shows that, historically, households in higher income brackets have seen their income rise faster than those in lower income brackets. The higher the income bracket, the higher the income growth rate. Since 1970, the top 5% of earning households in the country saw their income rise 1.5% faster than inflation every year, whereas the bottom quintile income barely caught up with inflation. Income inequality has structurally risen in the United States. The country is now meaningfully less equal compared to other developed countries such as the UK, Japan, Canda, or France.

More recently, however, there is a distinct new trend where the middle earners, instead of the bottom earners, are experiencing the slowest income growth. Households in the third and the fourth quintiles have seen the slowest income growth for a few years in a row compared to households in lower and higher quintiles. The middle class has become the weakest link in terms of earning growth potential.

To understand why this is the case, it helps to paint a picture of who the middle class is and how their lives have changed over the past decades. In 2021, the median annual household incomes before tax in the third and the fourth quintile brackets were US$73,000 and US$118,000 respectively. These income figures are in line with those of college-educated workers with a decade or two of working experience or those of skilled workers who may not be college educated but have acquired certain professional skills. Why are these middle-income workers comparatively worse off in recent years? Wages are the main source of income for middle-class families, compared to the affluent who get more of their income from capital. Data from the US Bureau of Economic Analysis shows that wages and salary as a percentage of GDP have fallen from 51.1% in 1970 to 46.9% in 2010 and 43.7% in 2022. As wages' slice of the overall GDP pie has shrunk over the years, a bigger share of the economic pie has been awarded to capital as higher profit and, as a result, higher stock price. In other words, the stock market has boomed, primarily benefiting the rich, but wages, the main source of income for the middle class, have risen less. A study by the Brookings Institution, a thinktank, suggests that substantially all of the middle-class household income gains since the 1970s have been due to longer hours worked and higher wages earned by women. In other words, the typical middle-income households have collectively worked a lot more hours, often with an additional earner in the family, to keep up with the income growth of other brackets. More time at work means less time spent with family and loved ones. It simply makes us more tired.

How will today's disruptive technologies change the income disparity across different income brackets?

Jobs that are least impacted are blue-collar manual jobs, which often sit in the lower quintile income brackets. Despite significant strides being made regarding machines performing more human tasks, machines still cannot match the dexterity of human beings in many manual jobs. Human hands have twenty-seven degrees of freedom, or "DOF," which is the measurement of possible positions or motions of a mechanical system in space. The higher the DOF, the more capable the mechanism is of complicated manipulations. The most common robotic hands have seven DOF, or about one-fourth the dexterity of a human hand. Robotic hands today can perform single-hand and specific tasks relatively well, such as painting a wall or moving an object from one place to another. However, they struggle to become general-purpose tools that can perform a wide range of tasks. It is difficult for robots to plan coordinated movements in sequence, which is essential to performing general-purpose tasks. The ability to have two robotic hands together is even further out of reach. No robotic hands can perform a simple two-handed task such as replacing the battery in a remote control. This is why machines have not yet been able to replace human hands in a lot of manual jobs. Amazon, one of the world's most successful technology companies, employs more than one million workers. The vast majority of them are packers, who are responsible for dealing with packages in warehouses. This line of work can be particularly hectic during the holiday season, and the company regularly experiences a shortage of packers during this time. In 2022, Amazon announced a plan to hire 150,000 workers in October, with an hourly wage of US$19 and a sign-on bonus of US$3,000 at select locations. That is equivalent to an extra 157 working hours paid up-front for a short-term employment contract that lasts only a month or two.

Disruptive technologies are more likely to change the way white-collar tasks are performed and how workers are rewarded accordingly.

White-collar jobs that require some professional training but lack high complexity and discretionary judgments are most likely to be negatively impacted. These routine white-collar jobs often fall within the middle-income brackets, and their income growth potential is likely limited. For example, twenty years ago, building a website was considered an advanced technology skill. Fast forward to today, one can set up a fully functioning e-commerce website through Shopify, an e-commerce platform, in a matter of minutes. It used to take a lot of time and effort for a person to learn a programming language in order to communicate with the machines. However, the barriers between machines and humans have broken down, thanks to technologies like large language models and natural language processing. People with no technological background are able to give commands in their native languages to machines, engaging them in various tasks.

At the same time, new technologies can enable many white-collar workers to become more productive, more creative, and more value added, which will translate into a higher income potential. A healthcare professional will spend less time performing voluminous routine tasks and instead focus on making important judgments in complicated circumstances where historical precedents may not be readily available. They may be willing to work for more years due to less burnout, advance their career further, and solve more complicated issues for patients and be rewarded accordingly for this. A freelance worker may not be able to afford an assistant, but they can now leverage the power of AI to get more done for less, boosting their earnings while controlling their costs. A gifted worker may have their talent enabled and augmented in a similar fashion to the way sales megastar Li Jiaqi ascended from a regular salesperson to one of the most prolific revenue generators in the Chinese retail industry. When an engineer is allowed to experiment without consequence in the virtual world, they are more likely to stumble upon solutions that produce revolutionary results. In all of these scenarios, the individual workers have been empowered to generate a lot more value-added professional output. They have gained more bargaining power over their employers and should therefore be rewarded accordingly.

Today's disruptive technologies will exert a large economic impact quickly. As established in earlier chapters, disruptive technologies will enlarge the overall economic pie by structurally enhancing economic growth. The first impact is a boost to productivity. Workers will likely perform many tasks differently in order to best incorporate these new productive tools. More can be done in fewer working hours. The second impact is a boost to consumer demand. Consumers will have better products to choose from and more time to consume. This sounds like a great plan of "work less, play more," but it may not be. Not every worker will adjust to the advent of new disruptive technologies. Not every business will survive the challenge. Not only are these new technologies characterized by the magnitude of their potential impact, but they have also been adopted at unprecedented speed. This means that workers and businesses will need to adjust much faster than previous rounds of technological innovations. We had seventy-five years to adjust when one hundred million people chose to adopt telephones and seven years to adjust when one hundred million people plugged into the world wide web. We had two months before ChatGPT reached one hundred million users.

The magnitude and speed at which today's disruptive technologies leave an impact mean it is more important than ever that mechanisms are put in place to cushion the impact on workers' income and households' living standards. Some workers and families may need short-term support until they retrain for new skills and jobs. Some may need longer-term support. Not every worker will adapt to the new technologies in a similar fashion, but it is imperative that these families are financially supported. The next generations in particular should be given a fair shot at the economic upsides of these technologies in the future. Average citizens need more generous income subsidies because their livelihoods may be impacted, either temporarily or permanently, despite the fact that society is collectively wealthier from techno-logical innovations. Economists have long agreed that higher income inequality raises social concerns and can hurt future economic growth. Reducing inequality strengthens people's sense of fairness, improves social cohesion, and encourages upward mobility. It is not a surprise that governments around the world collect more taxes (which is the main way governments redistribute wealth and address income inequality) as countries become richer. The total tax revenues in high-income countries like Denmark and France are close to 50% of the GDP, whereas the same figures in lower-income countries such as Mexico and Columbia are 20% of the GDP.

A more radical school of thought, which is not unpopular, is to adopt universal basic income. This calls for unconditional payment of a guaranteed income to all citizens, regardless of their job status and their existing salaries or wages. This will ensure that citizens will have a generous safety net to fall back on, giving them more flexibility to adapt to new jobs or simply live a basic life if they choose to. Elon Musk, a serial entrepreneur and one of the world's wealthiest people, said that new technologies such as automation will allow people to "do other things, more complex things, more interesting things . . . certainly more leisure time." Some of the old jobs will be eliminated because they can be performed more efficiently by machines. Musk concludes that "there is a pretty good chance we end up with a universal basic income."

Today's disruptive technologies will not eliminate the differences in income level or income growth rate. Instead, they will help motivated individuals open up more opportunities and potentially achieve a lot more by giving them productivity-boosting tools that are easy to access and multifunctional. Middle-income workers have a higher chance of experiencing faster income growth because they now have more resources on hand that they can use to accomplish more. With the right combination of motivation, effort, technology, and professional expertise, they may be able to grow their income level at a faster rate—not just faster than their peers but faster than people in higher income brackets. At a macroeconomic level, this can help promote upward social mobility from middle-income households to higher-income households.

The idea of creating a more equitable society is not that some people should never earn higher income or grow their income at a faster rate than others. Rather, it is about ensuring that the various income strata do not become so deeply entrenched that they are impossible to break through. A fair and equitable society is one where everyone has a fair shot at success and upward mobility. From this perspective, today's disruptive technologies can make a positive contribution.

CHAPTER **14**

NARROWING INCOME GAPS BETWEEN COUNTRIES IS HARDER THAN EVER

For decades, lower-earning economies have been expected to grow productivity faster than their richer peers. Higher productivity means more economic output and higher income, which helps to narrow the international income gap over time. Because poorer countries are, by definition, not at the forefront of technological developments, they have a vast backlog of innovations that can be readily adopted.

However, a recent study conducted by the World Bank shows that productivity growth in low-income countries has stagnated. Labor productivity in the poorest economies in the world is a mere 2% of the average economy. The pace of productivity convergence is so slow that at the current growth rate, it will take more than one hundred years to halve the existing productivity gap. This means the income gap between the rich and the poor countries will likely stay wide. Indeed, low-income countries have faced ongoing economic difficulties over the past few years due to the pandemic and the shock of higher food prices globally. In its 2023 World Economic Outlook, the International Monetary Fund, a United Nations financial agency, suggests that real GDP per capita in low-income countries shows no sign of converging with the level in advanced economies. Since the pandemic, the gap has only gotten wider.

There are several reasons why it is difficult to narrow the international income gap. One reason is that an abundance of cheap unskilled labor, which used to be a key competitive resource for lower-income countries, is less of a competitive advantage now. China's ascension to economic power in the early twenty-first century had everything to do with its vast and young population. Factory workers in their twenties with little prior working experience were willing to put in long, dreary hours churning out T-shirts, shoes, and furniture while getting paid well below the minimum wage of developed countries. Factories today have far fewer workers performing repetitive tasks on the production line because production has become more streamlined and machines have taken over a growing share of tasks. This is even more true for sectors that rely on digital technologies, which represent a growing share of the overall economy, and command a rising share of corporate profit. The marginal cost of production for a software company is near zero, which means cheap unskilled labor has little appeal to companies in these industries. It has become more difficult for developing countries to leverage their labor to catch up with the richer countries.

Another reason is that the entry barrier to the new generation of technologies has become higher than before. To start with, heavy up-front investments are needed to support the new generation of technologies. Building the hardware infrastructure for these technologies demands extensive investments. For example, the 5G network, which supports ultra-high-speed mobile connections, is essential to various technologies such as virtual reality, autonomous driving, and AI. The cumulative capital expenditure for the US to upgrade its mobile network has exceeded US$100 billion over the past few years. Even if lower-income countries can afford to pull together the financial resources, it has become a lot more difficult than before to replicate the technological know-how for the new generations of technologies. When Walmart developed an efficient "just-in-time" inventory management practice some decades ago, the technique became widely taught in business schools and implemented by companies around the world. It is difficult to copy the latest technologies. Take AI, for example. For most AI models, we are not able to understand how exactly they make their decisions. Large amounts of data are fed to the model for training and the model produces plausible results. However, neither the users nor the builders of these models are privy to the exact inner workings. This is known among AI researchers as the "black box problem." Many people know that Facebook uses an AI-based recommendation model to keep users engaged with its content. However, it is difficult for other companies in lower-income countries to replicate the workings of this model and recreate another Facebook.

Developed economies have a natural advantage over developing economies in providing skilled talent and innovation-friendly business environments. These two conditions are essential to realizing the significant growth potential of today's disruptive technologies. To start with, the level of education is generally higher in developed economies. According to data from the OECD, an intergovernmental organization, Korea, Canada, Japan, and Luxembourg are among the countries with the highest rate of tertiary education. More than 60% of the twenty-five-to-thirty-four-year-olds in these countries have received undergraduate and graduate educations. The same metric is less than 20% for South Africa, Indonesia, and Argentina. Not surprisingly, income levels are lower in these countries, and they have not been at the forefront of technological innovations. In addition, business environments that promote and protect innovation are critical. The World Intellectual Property Organization, a United Nations agency, publishes a Global Innovation Index each year. This index ranks countries by their capacities for and success in innovation. The 2022 index showed that the ten most innovative economies are Switzerland, the United States, Sweden, the United Kingdom, the Netherlands, Korea, Singapore, Germany, Finland, and Denmark. The ranking methodology takes into consideration inputs for innovation—including human capital, infrastructure, and the strength of institutions—as well as outputs of innovation, such as patents and new businesses per population. It is no surprise that the most innovative countries are richer regions where companies can access skilled talent, operate in business-friendly environments, and produce more innovative results.

Nonetheless, a select few emerging economies are well positioned to benefit from the new wave of technologies. India, for example, has a large quantity of skilled labor at an attractive cost, and a lot of the infrastructure is already in place for the world's most innovative businesses to operate there. The country has a well-established outsourcing industry, accounting for close to 10% of the country's GDP. Most of the current outsourcing businesses are in IT and customer services support that work in conjunction with overseas "front office" capabilities. The communication channels and the cultural practice of operating internationally have already been well tested. The country also offers skilled labor in large quantities, at a cheap cost, and in the right areas of focus. India awards seven million undergraduate degrees every year with an average starting salary of US$2,800. It is home to the largest population of engineers in the world. According to data from the United Nations, nearly one in every three college graduates worldwide who received their degrees in STEM subjects are from India. Many top executives from some of the world's most powerful tech companies received their undergraduate degrees in India and started their careers there. The list includes the incumbent CEO of Alphabet, Sundar Pichai; the incumbent CEO of Microsoft, Satya Nadella; and the incumbent chairman and CEO of IBM, Arvind Krishna. This shows that the vast human resources of the country can be highly adaptable to a global business environment, particularly in the technology business. A former executive at Tata Sons, a large Indian conglomerate, once claimed that no other nation in the world trains so many citizens in such a gladiatorial manner as India does and argued that the competition and chaos make adaptable problem solvers.

Over time, a new wave of technological changes can create a strong tailwind that can significantly accelerate the growth rate of lower-income countries and allow them to play catch-up with higher-income countries. Over the last few decades, Japan and China have been among the main beneficiaries of the technologies that enabled the smooth exchange of goods across countries. Global merchandise trade increased from less than 20% of global GDP after World War II to close to 50% by the turn of the century. The booming goods exports were supported by the proliferation of technologies such as telephones, the internet, software, and container and air freight, along with a complicated supply chain of industries, companies, and people working together around the world. For instance, Apple relies on the internet and software to keep information flowing across its supply chain. It uses air freight to fly the latest hardware models to its stores and consumers. They also lean heavily on supply chain partners like Foxconn, an electronics assembly company, which employs as many as two hundred thousand workers in a single iPhone factory in China. Looking ahead, India stands out as having great potential to benefit from the exchange of services across country borders. AI models need to be developed and maintained by adequate STEM talents. The quality of remote services can be improved when supported by augmented reality technologies. More productive activities may take place digitally, no longer constrained by the physical location of professionals.

In conclusion, today's disruptive technologies are unlikely to narrow the income gap between richer countries and poorer countries. Richer countries are likely to maintain their income lead because they have better-educated workforces and more innovation-friendly business environments, which are crucial conditions for the productivity boost associated with the disruptive technologies of today. Poorer countries will have a hard time catching up because cheap and abundant unskilled labor is less important a competitive advantage than before. New technologies also have higher barriers to entry in terms of capital investments and know-how, which will prevent poorer countries from replicating the success of richer countries. Nonetheless, a select few emerging countries stand to benefit from the new rounds of technological reshuffle. India, in particular, is uniquely positioned due to its large skilled workforce, competitive wage level, and specialty in STEM subjects. These labor force characteristics complement those in developed markets, such as the United States, which suffer from a shortage of available STEM talents. India's practice of working with international companies can also help them provide high-value-added services to the rest of the world. While the business environment in India may not be the same as it is in developed countries, they can nonetheless participate in and support the ongoing techno-logical shift in other parts of the world.

The wide income disparity between the richer and poorer countries deserves our attention. From a humanitarian perspective, a higher standard of living is the common pursuit of people around the world, and in poor societies, women, children, and the underprivileged are frequently the most vulnerable. From a pragmatic perspective, a stark contrast in the income levels across country borders can lead to social issues such as illegal immigration, human trafficking, international conflict, or even war. As individual workers, we should be more open to how people from different parts of the world can contribute to a collective productive process. Indeed, there are burgeoning areas where lower-income economies have been able to engage in the latest technologies. In Africa, data annotation and content moderation are two pillar use cases. Complex AI models rely on large quantities of data as input. Before this data can be consumed by machines, it needs to be cleaned to remove duplicates or invalid inputs, as well as be labeled before they can be useful to machines. For example, models trained for autonomous driving will need to be fed with training image sets in which images of road signs are clearly labeled. As more creative content becomes available, either generated by users or AI programs, there is a greater need for content moderation so that the appropriate content reaches the appropriate users. These tasks do not require a high level of prior training but are essential to powering the latest global technologies. This is an area where both the users and the providers of these services can benefit and, in doing so, narrow the economic gap between countries.

PART IV

MONEY AND WEALTH

Savings refers to the difference between how much is produced and how much is consumed. When a person earns more than they consume, this person is a net saver. They are accumulating wealth and getting richer. Wealth is savings accumulated over time.

Wealth takes many different forms. It can be stored as money or as investment instruments like stocks, bonds, properties, and art. Wealth is important because it helps us link production and consumption activities across different times, spaces, and people. A worker saves for their retirement fund so that it can be consumed decades later. A person may earn a salary in a higher-paying city and vacation in the countryside resort of a lower-income country. Parents may save money to pay for their children's tuition.

There is not a singular best way to manage wealth. It might be a safe idea to deposit the money into a bank, but that money risks losing value over time due to inflation. Investing in stocks and bonds may generate higher returns, but it's possible to lose those investments. New technologies have brought us new forms of investment destinations, including cryptocurrencies and digital art. Billionaires have been made quickly from these new instruments. But there have also been high-profile losses or even scams surrounding them.

Over time, these different instruments can produce very different outcomes. This chapter explores how new technologies impact our wealth. They do so by either impacting the value of existing investments or creating new forms of investments for us to participate in.

CHAPTER **15**

TECHNOLOGIES CREATE MORE WEALTH, BUT YOU WON'T ALWAYS MAKE MONEY BY INVESTING IN THEM

The fundamental economic rationale for adopting new technologies is to get more done for less. The theory of economics generally assumes that all entities, including individuals and corporations, are utility maximizing in our economic lives. Technologies that help businesses achieve more by creating more revenue for less cost improve earning ability and will be adopted. On the flip side, a salesperson would have a hard time trying to sell something that accomplishes less for more cost than the incumbent way of doing things because the change would undermine the rational economic interest of the potential clients. We adopted the railway because it helps us travel faster and further and bulk cargo can be transported over long distances at better costs than on horseback or boat. We adopted the internet because it helps us disseminate information faster at a lower cost. Emails, instant messages, documents, and files can arrive on the other end of the world almost instantly, and it is free. This enables business ideas to flow more easily between individuals, product designers to more readily incorporate client preferences, and exporters and importers to move goods across the globe faster.

How have technologies helped us get more done for less? They do so through rapid iteration of technical specifications and by enabling new business models that have not been possible under previous generations of technology. Amazon would not have been able to sell books online and reduce significant costs related to rentals, sales staff on the ground, and inventory maintenance if the internet had not existed and mobile technologies were not available at our fingertips. Technologies also help businesses scale up individual successes. This includes economically replicating or projecting existing business practices to many people over long distances. The sales miracle of Li Jiaqi as described in earlier chapters is an example of how one person's charisma can be augmented to rival the power of the largest incumbent players in this space. To quote Jim Kavanaugh, Chief Financial Officer of IBM, "The only deflationary force is technology. And technology now is a source . . . of sustainable, competitive advantage."

Further wealth is created when more is accomplished at a lower cost. When a company produces more for less, its revenue increases while its costs fall. As a result, the company generates more profit. The company's value is the sum of all future profits it will generate. When a person gets more done with less cost, they earn a higher income and spend less on the same set of goods. The difference can either be used to buy more goods and services, which would propel more economic activities and boost GDP growth, or be reserved as savings, which would create higher demand for investment instruments and drive up their prices. When an economy gets more done for less, people and capital will be drawn to the prospect of making a fortune in this economy, and it will grow faster. When expressed in macroeconomic terms, new technologies will boost the GDP growth rate without causing significantly higher rate of inflation. For example, as previously illustrated in earlier chapters, AI technologies alone are expected to accelerate the pace of the world's economic growth rate by half in the next decade or so.

However, it is important to note that investment prices do not always move in line with the growth potential of the underlying technologies. In other words, just because a promising set of technologies has been identified, it does not guarantee that investing in them will create more wealth.

Most financial assets are anticipatory in nature. This means that their investors do not simply price the assets based on the value they have already created. They also anticipate what value the technologies can potentially generate in the future. For nascent technologies that are exhibiting rapid growth adoptions, estimating their future growth and values can create a significant challenge for investors. The dot-com bubble in the late 1990s was accompanied by a period of genuine technological innovation, such as the widespread adoption of the internet. The market was so excited about the economic prospects of internet-based businesses that it was willing to overlook the simple fact that the vast majority of the NASDAQ companies then were loss making. The rapid share price appreciation is entirely based on the investors' anticipation that the companies will generate more income in the future.

There are also significant uncertainties regarding the validity of business models in the future. New technologies have different phases of becoming adopted. In the earlier phase, adventurous users and technology enthusiasts are the main adopters. The adoption grows at the highest rate from a very small base. If the technology is successful with the early users, it will enter the mainstream market, at which point larger businesses and mass-market entities start to incorporate these technologies. This is the part where the growth rate is slower due to a larger base effect, but as the technologies start to gain a mass following, this is where most of the profits will be made. Eventually, the technologies will reach a point of saturation where most users who find the product useful have adopted it already. Some technologies are able to keep growing at a high speed for a sustained period of time because they keep finding deeper market penetration and wider use cases. This was the case for Amazon when it evolved from being a dedicated online bookstore to selling a wide range of products and eventually developed into a cloud service provider. Other technologies reach their saturation point earlier than expected because new technologies have disrupted their marketplace. When DVDs were the prevailing format for storing videos, DVD rentals were a booming business for Blockbuster. However, when video streaming enabled the technological shift away from DVD, the glossy discs were quickly phased out, and Netflix became the mainstream way to access movies.

New and disruptive technologies are valuable because they enable us to get more done for less. When individuals, corporations, and economies are able to do so, they save more, generate more profit, and attract more people and capital flow. However, the value of our investments does not move in line with the state of technological developments. Identifying promising technologies does not guarantee a strong outcome. This is because investment values are often based on expectations, and expectations can become unrealistic when the market tries to estimate what a new technology's value will be in the far future, especially when it is in its nascent stage. There is also uncertainty as to the growth trajectory of new technologies. Some may sustain extraordinary growth for a long period of time, while others may become victims of disruptions by other upcoming technologies.

CHAPTER 16

BITCOIN IS MONEY, BUT NOT THE TYPE TO BUY GROCERIES WITH

New technologies do not just create more wealth in existing forms, such as stocks; they can also create new forms of wealth. Blockchain technologies and their related digital assets such as cryptocurrencies and NFTs are prime examples of this.

Bitcoin, the first cryptocurrency, was created after the 2008 financial crisis as an alternative to traditional banks and fiat money. The banking crisis had sown widespread distrust in the financial system, which was centered on large commercial banks and government agencies. Early proponents of Bitcoin declared that it would replace existing fiat money, which was based on a fragile financial system. That did not happen. Instead, over the last fifteen years, Bitcoin has grown alongside fiat money. While the vast majority of the money and wealth in the world is still based on fiat currencies, Bitcoin has proven its ability to serve the two main purposes of money: storage of wealth and medium of transactions.

There are two main conditions for something to be considered a meaningful form of wealth storage. First, it should preserve value when compared to other forms of wealth, such as the US dollar, the world's most widely accepted fiat currency. The first meaningful trading of the cryptocurrency against the US dollar took place in 2010, when its value jumped from a fraction of a penny to US$0.08. Since then, the value of Bitcoin has climbed at a dizzying speed. Bitcoin price reached its all-time high in November 2021, when the coin traded at over US$65,000 per coin. At the time of writing, the price of Bitcoin is US$30,200. It has gone up over three hundred times over the past ten years, which translates to an annualized growth rate of 79%.

Second, a meaningful form of wealth storage should be widely held so that many people recognize its value. This is indeed the case for bitcoins. An estimated forty-six million Americans own bitcoins, according to the New York Digital Investment Group, a Bitcoin company. This represents 13% of the country's total population and nearly 20% of its adult population. Cryptocurrencies are widely held by people around the world and across income levels. In the United Arab Emirates, a wealthy country, nearly 30% of its residents own cryptocurrencies. Countries with crypto ownership over 10% also include the Philippines, a low-income country, war-torn Ukraine, and Venezuela, where over 90% of its population lives in poverty.

In addition to being a form of wealth storage, Bitcoin is also a transaction currency for goods and services. On May 22, 2010, Bitcoin enthusiast Laszlo Hanyecz made history by paying 10,000 bitcoins, worth about US$40 at the time, for two large Papa John's pizzas.

Hanyecz wanted to prove that Bitcoin is real money that can be used to purchase goods. He succeeded in completing the first real-world Bitcoin transaction. The only caveat is that the same number of bitcoins would be worth well over US$200 million by today's valuation, which can buy ten million large Papa John's pizzas. Bitcoin Pizza Day is observed every year on May 22 to commemorate this somewhat costly anecdote in cryptocurrency history. Papa John's is not the only mainstream business to accept the cryptocurrency. Microsoft started accepting bitcoins as payments as early as 2014, only a few years after the birth of cryptocurrencies. Starbucks started accepting bitcoins in 2018. Its coffee ordering app integrates with bitcoin wallets to help transactions go smoothly. Tesla began accepting bitcoins for its electric vehicles in February 2021 following a high-profile announcement by CEO Elon Musk. However, this decision was reneged a few months later. The company, citing environmental concerns related to Bitcoin mining and transaction activities, said it is considering other cryptocurrencies with higher energy efficiency.

Ironically, Bitcoin's popularity as a personal investment destination has directly contributed to the fact that few real-world transactions are actually denominated in bitcoins. This is because Bitcoin's appreciation against everything else—including US dollars, pizzas, cars, and stocks—has been so rapid that the best thing to do with bitcoins is to simply hold onto them. In other words, Bitcoin preserves wealth so well that it discourages people from letting it go in exchange for goods and services.

To understand the macroeconomic implications of this, let us conduct a thought experiment. Imagine a fictional Coinland, where residents have fully adopted Bitcoin as the only form of currency. People hold bitcoins in their savings accounts, they are paid salaries in bitcoins, and all transactions are denominated in bitcoins. In 2010, a Papa John's pizza cost 5,000 bitcoins, as Mr. Hanyecz found out on the inaugural Bitcoin Pizza Day. In 2023, the same Papa John's pizza cost 0.001 bitcoin, based on a market price of US$30,000 per bitcoin. The price of pizzas denominated in bitcoin has shrunk by 69% per year over these last fourteen years. And the prices of everything else, denominated in bitcoin, have done similar things. Constantly falling prices in local currency create a significant economic incentive for all residents to postpone any purchases as far out as possible. Why buy a car today for one hundred bitcoins if it costs only thirty-one bitcoins next year or nine bitcoins the year after? If every citizen of Coinland rationally chooses to postpone their purchases, on an aggregate level there will be few economic activities conducted, few jobs created, and few entrepreneurial efforts. The Coinland economy will simply be dead.

The Coinland example illustrates why, from an economic perspective, Bitcoin is not ready to become a mainstream transaction currency despite being widely accepted as a personal investment destination. A transaction currency should be relatively stable in value so that both parties in the transaction feel like they are exchanging values on fair terms.

Looking ahead, Bitcoin is likely to continue serving the role of wealth storage much better than it does the role of transaction currency. It is already a popular form of retail investment holding for average households and individuals around the world. Most of these investors are not shunning away from the mainstream financial market, as the creator of Bitcoin had originally envisioned. They instead use the cryptocurrency as a way to diversify their wealth holdings beyond traditional financial instruments such as stocks, funds, and deposits and participate in the potential appreciation of the currency's value. They may occasionally pay for a Starbucks coffee on their app with bitcoin just because they can, but it is unlikely that they will use bitcoin for most of their transactions.

CHAPTER **17**

SUPPLY AND DEMAND DETERMINE THE PRICE OF MONEY, JUST LIKE EVERYTHING ELSE

Basic economic law states that prices of goods and services are driven by the relative balance between supply and demand. The lower the supply is relative to demand, the higher the prices. This law applies to the value of money too. The more money is supplied, the less valuable each unit of money becomes. In this section, we will discuss the supply and demand of cryptocurrencies and how those impact their prices. We will first compare the supply mechanisms of different forms of money to illustrate how they inspire drastically different levels of trust in their users. We will then dive into what drives the demand for crypto-currencies and use a case study to illustrate how to identify a speculative price bubble in cryptocurrency.

MONEY SUPPLY—BITCOIN SUPPLY PEAKS IN ONE HUNDRED YEARS. THE US DOLLAR? NEVER.

Classic macroeconomic theories state that the supply of money should broadly match the needs of the underlying economy. This is why more money gets printed every year to keep up with the natural growth in economic activities and maintain a healthy level of price inflation. An economy that manufactures and sells 100 cars the first year and 110 cars the following year would need 10% more money each year because 10% more economic activities are taking place.

In addition, central banks usually like to create a moderate level of price appreciation. A car that costs 100 units of local currency today is likely to cost 102 a year later. This creates a mild incentive for buyers to make their purchases at their earliest convenience, but it does not erode the purchasing power of wage earners too quickly. Central banks around the world typically manage their money supplies to be broadly in line with the nominal GDP growth of their countries.

Indeed, the growth of money supply in the US has averaged 7% per year since the 1960s, which is broadly in line with the expansion rate of the US economy. It can be problematic when the money supply severely deviates from the pace of economic growth. For example, in response to the COVID-19 pandemic, the US government created extraordinary stimulus packages in 2020, including direct cash payments to citizens, unemployment benefits, and substantial loans and grants to small businesses, schools, and hospitals. The money supply in the US shot up by 26%. The abnormal supply created disorderly price movements. The price of used cars, for example, surged by more than 50% in the following year.

However, the money supply of cryptocurrencies is not designed with mainstream macroeconomic frameworks in mind.

The bitcoin supply is algorithmically determined with an absolute supply ceiling and a fixed schedule of issuance. Bitcoin is designed to reach its supply limit of twenty-one million on October 5, 2138. Before then, under the Bitcoin protocol, a new block of bitcoin transaction records is added every ten minutes. For every 210,000 blocks created, which happens approximately every four years, the reward for adding a block is reduced by half. It becomes incrementally harder to earn bitcoins as time goes by, until they reach their supply limit more than a century away from today.

The supply of Ethereum, the second-most-valuable cryptocurrency, does not have an upper limit. Instead, each year, the Ethereum supply grows at a maximum of 18 million ETH. This means that its maximum growth rate will gradually decline because the existing money base is getting bigger while the increments at which the supply increases stay the same.

The difference in money supply accumulates and it can lead to very significant differences in total money outstanding over time. Over the last ten years, the US money supply has increased by 100%, according to data from the Federal Reserve. The supply of bitcoins has grown by 50%, and the supply of Ethereum by 67%. Over the next ten years, if the Federal Reserve continues to manage its currency in a similar fashion, which the world expects it will, the US money supply will again grow by 100%. Bitcoin's total supply, however, will grow by only 5% cumulatively as per its decelerating growth mechanism. The maximum supply of Ethereum will grow a maximum of 150% cumulatively. In other words, over time, we will get a lot more US dollars and Ethereum than bitcoins due to the different design of the money supply.

There is no best way to design a money supply. A conventional fiat money supply can adapt to the underlying economic conditions but requires significant judgment and competency by central banks and authorities. The supply of bitcoins is a simple mathematical algorithm that will not be tampered with by any personal, political, or business interests. It was designed as a counterproposal to developed world fiat money in one of the darkest moments of modern economic history, the Global Financial Crisis in 2008. At the time, major banks were breaking down, businesses were severely affected, and many people had lost their life savings and houses. Trust in the financial system was deeply shaken. The plain and mechanical nature of Bitcoin was a stark alternative to mainstream finance at the time. Fortunately, much of the faith in the conventional monetary system has been restored in the years following the financial crisis. The money supply design of cryptocurrencies has not replaced the work of central banks but has instead complemented them by providing people with an alternative way to manage their money.

When authorities do not manage their own fiat money in good faith, it can lead to a serious economic and humanitarian crisis. Venezuela is an example of this. In Venezuela, inflation has been out of control for a decade. Annual inflation exceeded 1,000,000% in 2018, and the local currency, the bolivar, lost 90% of its value every five months. While the decline in oil prices was an initial shock for this oil-exporting country, corruption and a lack of government discipline caused this problem to persist and deepen. Local central banks faced political pressure to keep printing money to fund government spending, which was then frequently misappropriated. High inflation rendered household savings worthless and severely disrupted the normal order of economic activities. By 2017, hunger was so widespread that nearly 75% of the population had lost at least nineteen pounds. A United Nations report estimated that 94% of Venezuelans lived in poverty in 2019, and almost 20% of Venezuelans had left their home country by 2021.

Money, at its core, is trust. Modern fiat money is backed by nothing but the trustworthiness of its issuing authorities, which are the central banks appointed by the government. Average citizens who hold this money place their trust in the competency and the goodwill of the central banks to manage monetary policies well. They trust that the authorities will not print too much money, which would cause inflation and the erosion of their purchasing power. They trust that the authorities will not print too little money, which would inhibit economic activities and cause unemployment rates to rise. One significance of cryptocurrencies is that they created a decentralized framework of money that does not rely on human judgments to function well. This is a meaningful alternative for average citizens who have neither the powerful position nor the professional expertise to decide the best monetary pathway. In March 2023, days after the failure of Silicon Bank, a midsize commercial bank in California, bitcoin prices went up by almost 50%. A small confidence crisis in US banks caused people to flock to an alternative to the conventional financial industry. Fortunately, the authorities acted promptly to avoid losses for average individuals and households and swiftly restored faith in the banking system.

MONEY DEMAND—WHAT REALLY DRIVES IT?

The first driver of demand for any currency, fiat or crypto, is the genuine demand to purchase goods or assets denominated in that currency. If country A produces a highly sought-after type of machinery, people from all over the world would exchange their own currency for currency A in order to purchase such a machine. Demand for currency A would go up because the rest of the world demands products denominated in currency A. In a cryptocurrency setting, the mechanism is similar. Ethereum, for example, is needed to conduct any transactions on the Ethereum blockchain. Anyone who wishes to utilize the Ethereum blockchain for its smart contract feature or to purchase an NFT, most of which are based on the Ethereum blockchain, will exchange their own money for Ethereum. The more widely used the underlying blockchain environment and its products and features, the higher the demand for its cryptocurrency and the higher the prices of the cryptocurrency.

The second driver of demand is investment returns, including interest incomes and gains from price appreciation. Fiat money generates interest rates. In 2023, US dollar deposits offer interest rates of nearly 5%, which is an attractive return compared to Japanese yen deposits, which yield zero interest income. People may also choose to hold a currency speculatively because they expect it will appreciate in price against other forms of currency. As illustrated in an earlier chapter, since its early trading days in 2010, Bitcoin has risen spectacularly in value against every single major currency in the world. The value of a bitcoin has gone up more than three hundred times over the past ten years, which translates to an annualized growth rate of 79%. This has fueled speculative interest, drawing in people who would also like to partake in future price appreciations.

The third and most important driver of demand for a currency is the innovation and productivity of the underlying economy. Numerous researchers from central banks and various academic institutions have found that innovation leads to productivity gains, which are associated with a higher rate of GDP growth, a higher level of income, and an increase in the appreciation of local currency. When China joined the World Trade Organization in 2001, the country experienced a huge productivity boost from being exposed to large export markets, abundant foreign direct investments, and transferable knowledge of production technologies and business management. Over the next fifteen years, the country's GDP grew at an average of 10% per year while its currency, the Chinese Yuan, appreciated by 28%.

Similarly, the long-term driver of demand for cryptocurrencies is their ability to create genuine productivity gains by solving real problems for people. Bitcoin offers a solution to the confidence crisis in the traditional financial system by decentralizing monetary frameworks and encrypting money transactions in a secure manner. Ethereum provides a solution to the enforceability of complex contracts by automating customizable smart contracts on the blockchain. If the underlying crypto environment provides unique and effective solutions, the technologies will be structurally adopted over time. In other words, by creating a genuine productivity gain, the underlying digital economy of cryptocurrencies will be more attractive, and people will want to participate in these activities through cryptocurrencies. This would be the long-term anchor of cryptocurrency demand and value.

Nonetheless, speculative forces can sometimes win over long-term structural drivers for a short period of time when new technologies emerge rapidly and market sentiments are bubbly. In times like this, it can feel like the prices of the hottest cryptocurrencies, regardless of whether they serve any genuine purposes, can rise indefinitely. The boom and bust of the game Axie Infinity and its native currency tell a spectacular story of what happens when the value of a currency isn't backed by a genuine demand for goods and services.

Axie Infinity is a blockchain-based video game developed by Vietnamese studio Sky Mavis in 2018. The game's main characters are cute pet-like

creatures called Axies. Axies are NFTs, or unique
digital art, that can be bought from the game's
marketplace. To play the game, each player needs to
form a team of at least three Axies to battle against
another team of three. The winner of the battle is
rewarded with the in-game cryptocurrency Small Love
Potion, or SLP. SLP can then be used to breed new
Axies, which can then be retained by the player or
sold in the in-game marketplace.

Axie Infinity gained tremendous popularity shortly
after its launch because it was marketed as a "play to
earn" game. The investment pitch was simple: invest
in three Axies NFTs, earn SLP cryptocurrency by
winning battles, breed more Axie NFTs, and sell them
for higher prices. By summer 2021, this simple game
drew around one million daily players and became the
biggest crypto app on the Ethereum blockchain. Axie
NFT prices were going up, SLP prices were going up,
and they reinforced each other.

There was just one problem: most players did not
enjoy playing the game. They played as a way to make
a living because they were hoping the prices of their
digital assets, including both the Axie NFTs and SLP
cryptocurrencies, would rise indefinitely. The crowd of
speculative players was mainly from two low-income
countries, the Philippines and Ecuador, where
people's cost of time is relatively low. At its height, the

lowest price for an Axie was US$340, which means that it costs over US$1,000 to form a team of three to play the game with. In 2021, the average annual family income in the Philippines was less than US$6,000 according to the local statistics authority. Do these people really benefit from spending two months of their entire family income to play a game they did not even enjoy? Clearly not. Axies and SLPs were instruments of one-way speculation, making it ripe for collapse. By the summer of 2022, the price of Axies had dropped to $6 and the market price of SLPs had fallen by 99%.

The rise and fall of Axie Infinity prove that while self-reinforcing price speculation may drive significant appreciation for a short period of time, over the long term, the underlying cryptocurrency must demonstrate it has created a genuine use case and real demand. Often, it takes a pause and a commonsense check to judge whether a new crypto-currency and its environment are serving a meaningful purpose. If there is no genuine innovation and demand, the currency can ultimately prove a lot less valuable than short-term speculators would think.

CHAPTER **18**

ICOS ARE NOT IPOS— THEY CAN BE GOOD OPPORTUNITIES, OR THEY CAN BE SCAMS

As a relatively young form of financial instruments, cryptocurrencies offer a creative way for companies and communities to attract capital, especially if their businesses are operating in the digital economy. The process of introducing a new cryptocurrency, often referred simply to as "coins," is called an Initial Coin Offering, or an ICO. Both the name and the practice of ICOs draw inspiration from the more established concept of an Initial Public Offering, or IPO. An IPO is where a company becomes publicly listed on a stock exchange and their equity shares are offered to investors in the general public for the first time.

Binance Coin, or BNB, is the cryptocurrency issued by Binance, a popular cryptocurrency exchange. It allows owners to get discounts on trading fees on the Binance exchange and subscribe to new, exclusive coin listings on Binance. By market cap, BNB is the fourth-largest cryptocurrency in the world, ranking only after Bitcoin, Ethereum, and Tether, which is a cryptocurrency whose value is explicitly linked to the US dollar. BNB was initially introduced to the general public in 2017 via an ICO process. Over time, as more people traded their cryptocurrencies on Binance and more new cryptocurrencies became listed for trading there, BNB price grew phenomenally, up from less than US$1 at ICO to US$240 at the time of writing.

The ICO process does bear some similarity to the IPO process. To general public investors, they both represent an opportunity to invest in something that has been previously unavailable. It can generate significant returns over time. To the issuing company, an ICO represents a way to raise capital from the general public and share economic incentives with them. To continue with the previous example, the ICO of BNB took place during a nine-day period in the summer of 2017. After the ICO, angel investors in Binance retained 10% of the total supply of BNB, management kept 40%, and the general public acquired the remaining 50%. In a typical IPO process, companies sell at least 20% of their total shares or tokens to the general public as "free float." Large shareholders, management, and employees often choose to retain a substantial stake in the company even after the IPO. The allocation of the new financial instruments bears similarity to one another.

However, ICOs are certainly not IPOs, and it is crucial that average investors understand the differences.

To start with, an equity stock represents ownership in a company, and a cryptocurrency does not. When you own a share of a company's stock, you essentially have an ownership claim over the company, all of its assets and operations, and all of its current and future profits. Accumulate over 50% ownership of the company's total stocks, and you are said to have gained financial "control" over the company. You can make plans for the business, distribute or reinvest its profit, change its board members, or even sell the company to another buyer if you like. Cryptocurrencies, however, do not give their owners a share of the issuing company. They instead tend to serve a specific utility like, in the case of BNB, reducing transaction costs on the trading platform of Binance. These utility functions are usually designed by the issuing company and are linked to that business. In other words, you can think of cryptocurrencies as game tokens issued by developers. Players can use them to purchase and upgrade their avatars, but they do not represent any ownership of the game developing business itself. A company typically issues only one type of equity share because the ownership of the company is a singular form of asset. However, there is no limit to how many different cryptocurrencies a company can issue. It is entirely possible that a company can issue a new line of cryptocurrency for different functions and different lines of business. No company ownership is at stake in the case of cryptocurrency.

Another key differentiating factor is how mature the underlying businesses are at the time of ICOs and IPOs. The median time between the founding of a company and it becoming publicly listed through an IPO is eleven years, according to data from NASDAQ. Before their IPO, companies typically have gone through rounds of private investments, usually led by venture capital and private equity firms, which means their business and financial profiles have come under the scrutiny of many professional investors. On the other hand, an ICO can happen as early as a few months after the start of a blockchain project. Bitcoin was released as open-source code on the blockchain merely three months after its initial concept was born. From that day on, Bitcoin was open to be owned by anyone in the public. BNB was initially offered to its investors in 2017, shortly after the company was founded that same year. The ICO offering helped Binance raise US$15 million from general public investors, even though the company had little track record of either running a business or generating a profit. It is a lucky coincidence that Binance subsequently blossomed into one of the largest exchanges for cryptocurrencies in the world with a revenue of more than US$12 billion in 2022. There are many other ICOs that were barely backed by a legitimate business or even a plausible plan for commercial success.

For now, regulatory and compliance hurdles are significantly lower for ICOs than for IPOs. Publicly listing stocks on an exchange is a highly regulated practice. If a company plans to conduct a registered public offering in the US, it must file a registration statement with the US Securities and Exchange Commission (SEC) before offering its securities for sale. The company may not proceed with the IPO until the SEC declares the registration statement effective. A typical IPO process takes months, if not years, and costs millions of US dollars. It requires extensive collaboration among investment bankers, auditors, and lawyers. The company must show a convincing track record of operation, and a minimum of three years of operating and financial information is shared with the general public.

On the other hand, so far, ICOs operate with limited regulatory oversight. When an ICO is conducted on a centralized exchange like Binance, the exchange conducts basic background checks and antifraud measures to reduce the risk of investor loss. Nonetheless, the role of crypto exchanges in ICOs is not the same as the role played by regulators for IPOs. There is a fundamental conflict of interest at play. Exchanges make money from listing and trading more cryptocurrencies and therefore should not be viewed as an impartial regulator like the SEC. When an ICO is conducted on a decentralized exchange, there is even less scrutiny. Anyone is allowed to list new coins and provide liquidity on any coin trades. Many rely on online forums and social media to market their coins, and the risk of fraud is even higher.

There are ongoing efforts by regulators around the world to address the potential conflict of interest and the highly speculative nature of cryptocurrency offerings.

In September 2017, China became the first major country to ban ICOs outright. The regulator voiced concerns that some ICOs are financial scams and pyramid schemes. This caution was echoed by Singapore's monetary authority, which issued a statement shortly after China's ban, stating that "ICOs are vulnerable to money laundering and terrorist financing risks."

In the United States, the SEC is also proposing that cryptocurrency offerings be placed under more regulatory scrutiny, although this idea has met pushback from the crypto community. All crypto-currency sales are subject to the Howey Test, named after a US Supreme Court case from 1946, to assess whether the cryptocurrency instrument constitutes a "security." If the cryptocurrency is indeed considered a security, its sales should be regulated directly by the SEC and subject to a lot more regulation than they are currently. In July 2023, the New York district court made an important ruling regarding the regulatory status of cryptocurrencies. The court ruled, by split decision, that the sale of the cryptocurrency Ripple should be subject to SEC regulations when sold to large institutional investors but not subject to SEC regulations when sold to small retail investors. The somewhat conflicting decision showcases just how complicated it is to regulate new financial inventions and how much discretionary judgment is needed in the changing landscape of cryptocurrency regulations.

In summary, ICOs are not IPOs. Unlike stocks, cryptocurrencies do not represent ownership in the issuing company. They are often offered by young companies that have limited track records. Regulatory oversight is much less present in cryptocurrencies than in other securities. A 2018 study by the *Wall Street Journal* found that one in five ICOs showed "red flags" of potentially being a scam. Individual investors should be mindful of both the potential upsides as well as the downsides and risks when investing in ICOs.

CHAPTER **19**

HIGHER IS NOT ALWAYS BETTER—HISTORY HAS A LESSON FOR TODAY'S CRYPTO INVESTORS

This section takes a long-term economic view and explains that, while higher prices may create more short-term gain for cryptocurrency investors today, they are not always better for the long-term development of the technology. Cryptocurrency prices move with the perceived popularity and usefulness of its underlying technology. The more widely adopted the underlying technologies are, the more they are able to provide utility to end users and the higher the prices of their cryptocurrencies will be. However, short-term speculation of cryptocurrency prices can become so extreme that their price movements may lose sight of these fundamental factors and actually hinder the adoption of their underlying technologies. This becomes particularly problematic when the developer companies are incentivized to drive up the price of the cryptocurrencies to reap short-term capital gains.

Early cryptocurrencies were designed with the core philosophy of decentralization in mind. The blockchain creates a peer-to-peer network that bypasses financial intermediaries and authorities. A consensus voting mechanism based on a simple majority is used to make all decisions on the blockchain, from transaction verifications to underlying software changes. It takes 50.1% of all holders of the cryptocurrency to make any major decisions. The holders of these cryptocurrencies are diversified enough that the transaction records and decisions on the blockchain cannot be easily controlled or manipulated by a small group of interest parties, and the power in the blockchain stays decentralized. For example, the Ethereum Foundation, the main developer of the Ethereum cryptocurrency and its blockchain, is a nonprofit organization that retains less than 1% of the total Ethereum supply. The Ethereum Foundation does not seek to direct the future trajectory of Ethereum and instead sets its mission to support the Ethereum blockchain and its ecosystem.

However, this initial vision for decentralization is lost in the design of many subsequent cryptocur-rencies, especially ones that are issued by for-profit companies. Many companies have opted to retain a substantial stake in the cryptocurrency they issue to better align with the economic incentives between the company and the coin holders. In the example of BNB, founders and management retained 40% of the coins at the time of ICO in 2017. At the time of writing, 22% of all BNB remains "out of circulation," which means they are not held by the general public. Similar to Ethereum, BNB has a consensus-based mechanism through which more ownership of the coins gives its holders more decision-making votes. This means the company management wields substantial power over the blockchain and can implement changes that will cause its value to fluctuate. In other words, the BNB ecosystem is much more dependent on the goodwill and competence of the project developer compared to a truly decentralized ecosystem such as Ethereum.

If we draw an analogy between these digital economies, denominated in their indigenous crypto-currencies, and the actual economy, denominated by fiat currencies, we may find conflicts of interest in many areas. The for-profit companies that issue cryptocurrencies are also simultaneously their largest owners. The same companies set the rules on how coins can be used and how business can be conducted. It would be the equivalent of one entity in the United States acting simultaneously as the chair of the Federal Reserve (decides how much US dollars to print), the richest person (owns most US dollars), and the president of the country (commands the highest executive power). This would be a preposterous combination of power. Some of these blockchain developers are singularly incentivized to bid up the price of their cryptocurrencies, which directly translates into a higher personal net worth, without considering whether the price appreciation is supported by genuine demand, whether it is sustainable, or whether it is good for the long-term health of the projects they are promoting.

At the core of this conflict of interest is the rule that higher is not always better. Higher cryptocurrency prices may be good for the personal wealth of major owners, but they can hinder the development of the underlying technology. Cryptocurrencies represent digital costs incurred to conduct various activities in the blockchain environment, and a sustainable cost is needed to encourage long-term adoption of the technology. On the Ethereum blockchain, for example, the fees that are required to execute a transaction regardless of its success are denominated in Ethereum. These are called gas fees. This name is designed to evoke the analogy between Ethereum, a form of utility cost on its synonymous blockchain, and gasoline fees, which are the utility costs of operating a car.

Cryptocurrency investors today may look back on the history of the petroleum industry for a relevant lesson. Early speculation on a nascent technology led to skyrocketing prices for a while, but the costs of the technology must settle down to a reasonable level before they can be widely adopted. The modern petroleum industry began in 1859, when oil drilling techniques were developed in Pennsylvania. This technological breakthrough fueled significant investments and established petroleum as a major industry. Between 1861 and 1865, oil prices shot up from below US$26 per barrel to over US$160 per barrel (2023 USD equivalent). Ironically, oil had not yet been discovered for its biggest modern use as a transportation fuel because cars were not invented until 1886 - two decades later! The primary use of oil at the time was to light lamps. Nonetheless, people were excited about the future of using oil as an energy source, and speculators drove up the price of oil rapidly in the early days. Almost two hundred years later, oil in its various forms, such as gasoline, diesel, or kerosene, is the largest source of energy and the number one transportation fuel for the entire world. However, the price of oil, a utility cost paid for by many households and businesses, is at ~US$80 per barrel, or about half of the price nearly two hundred years ago. Elevated oil prices set back its demand, and those early speculators who poured into an unproven technology at whatever cost suffered financial losses. For blockchain technologies to be more widely adopted, it's possible that cryptocurrency prices as a cost for utilizing the technology may have to come down a lot. Investors should be aware of the risk of entering into the speculation of an early technology.

CHAPTER **20**

WE SHOULD FOCUS ON THE INTRINSIC VALUE, RATHER THAN THE HYPE, OF DIGITAL ART

In addition to being the home of cryptocurrencies, blockchain technologies have also enabled NFTs to be safely stored, exhibited, and traded. Prior to the advent of blockchain technologies, digital art formats, whether they were paintings, music, or videos, were often challenged by the issue of piracy. Because the marginal cost of making an additional digital copy is near zero, there is a significant economic incentive to illegally disseminate these digital objects. It is also difficult to claim full ownership of a digital asset. For example, another person may have a digital copy of the same painting stored on their hard drive, and it is hard to tell who is the real owner. Blockchain technology solves this issue because it can keep the full transaction records of NFTs. This can be used to easily authenticate the ownership history of these digital objects. By ensuring the right lineage of these objects, the technology protects intellectual property in the digital world. It helps creators achieve better economic outcomes by ensuring their products cannot be easily duplicated. It also helps owners of these assets appreciate the value of their belongings, knowing their exact history and scarcity in the world.

Blockchain technology creates artificial scarcity in the digital world. Unique digital assets can be stored as NFTs on the blockchain, where all their production and transaction records are documented with permanent and unalterable records. Any copies of digital assets that do not have proper blockchain provenance would not be considered authentic. Remember the rule of supply and demand. By setting man-made limits to the supply of authenticated digital art, blockchain technology is an effective tool to instill the scarcity of digital objects in collectors' minds.

The Bored Ape Yacht Club, or simply Bored Ape, is an NFT collection that has garnered significant interest from digital art collectors. The collection consists of ten thousand unique, algorithmically generated pictures of cartoon apes that are recorded on the Ethereum blockchain. In 2021, one of the pictures, Bored Ape Yacht Club #8817, sold at Sotheby's metaverse digital art marketplace for US$3.4 million. This bored ape has sleepy eyes, a party horn in his mouth, and a wool turtleneck. The most unique features of this bored ape are that it has gold fur, shared by only 0.88% of other apes in the collection, and that it has a bored party horn in its mouth, shared by only 0.46% of other apes. While the design and the probability of these features follow entirely arbitrary rules made by the designer, they inspire an artificial sense of scarcity in these digital objects. The blockchain technology ensures that these arbitrary rules are not to be violated for the authentic collection, and the NFTs were able to fetch high prices in the market.

To be clear, the practice of creating artificial scarcity is not a new invention. The luxury goods industry has long embraced artificial scarcity as a lucrative business practice. Hermès, a French luxury fashion company, manufactures premium leather handbags. Prices start at $10,000 for popular models such as the Birkin bag, and they reach north of US$1 million for rare designs. The company caps the volume growth of handbag production at 6% to 7% annually, despite strong demand, indicating that they prefer to keep customers on a waiting list rather than accelerate production. The perceived value of these handbags has far exceeded that of an average purse or even the fine craftsmanship involved in making them. They have become status symbols that blatantly hint that their owners belong to a highly affluent social class.

However, the reality is that only a handful of companies are able to command a persistent luxury premium and operate a profitable business based on artificial scarcity. Most people carry on with their lives using reasonably priced bags without ever needing a product from Hermès. The real question for the artificially scarce NFTs is whether they offer such unique values to their customers that they can be viewed as exclusive collectibles, rather than something that can be easily substituted by another similar digital creation.

Some artists have already begun to challenge the boundaries of digital and physical arts. Damien Hirst, one of the most successful living artists, made headlines in 2022 when he publicly burned millions of dollars' worth of his own art from a London gallery after selling copies of them as NFTs. The artwork was part of a collection of ten thousand pieces called *The Currency*. Each one is an original piece made by Hirst, individually numbered and uniquely titled with the artist's favorite lyrics and chosen by a machine-learning algorithm. Hirst sold each piece in *The Currency* for US$2,000, and each buyer had to specify whether they wanted a physical copy or an NFT. If they chose the physical copy, the digital copy would be erased. If they chose the digital copy, the physical copy would be publicly set on fire and permanently destroyed. Hirst said burning his own art pieces was "completing the transformation of these physical artworks into NFTs . . . The value of art, digital or physical . . . will be transferred to the NFT as soon as they are burnt." This public affair was designed to make a statement about art transcending its physical shape and form. The NFT copies generated, the physical copies burned, the act of an artist setting his own creation on fire, and the news headlines it generated were all part of the artistic experience. In the end, his buyers were pretty evenly split in their preference for physical versus digital art. Of the

10,000 buyers, 5,149 buyers opted for the physical version, while the remaining 4,851 chose NFTs.

As we continue to embrace more digital objects and experiences, it is helpful to remember that human beings are natively spatial and physical beings. Some in-person experiences and habits are hard to mimic virtually. The ability to see, feel, hear, and touch defines our human experiences and habits and gives rise to some of our most profound personal moments. The joy of holding a loved one in your arms, the touch of soft sand on a breezy beach, and the awe at seeing Michelangelo's painting on the Sistine Chapel ceiling with your own eyes are spatial and sensory experiences that are impossible to replicate fully in the digital world. Some human experiences and habits are fundamentally different in the digital versus the physical world.

Decentraland is an online platform that tries to replicate the real estate industry in a virtual space. The platform allows users to buy virtual land, construct virtual buildings, and sell virtual fashion items designed for digital avatars. In November 2021, a patch of virtual land located on Fashion Street, a large shopping district within Decentraland, sold for a record US$2.4 million. The land measured 6,090 virtual square feet and cost more than the average home in Manhattan or San Francisco. Its buyer, token.com, said it intended to use the space to host digital fashion events and sell virtual clothing for avatars. However, recent estimates by various third-party sources suggest that the daily active user count in Decentraland, which has a vast land area of over two hundred million virtual square feet, is below one thousand, which makes it a virtual ghost town. The buyer of the expensive virtual storefront has probably sold few virtual T-shirts, and the property prices have suffered a sharp correction from their once lofty heights. The assumption that people, through their digital avatars, will visit one shop front after another on a virtual main street, browsing for clothes the same way they do in physical malls, is simply unrealistic.

New technologies have given rise to new forms of collectible assets and a new medium of art. Blockchain technology allows digital art to be created and exchanged in a fully documented manner to ensure authenticity and ownership history. This protects artists' economic interests and helps buyers establish undisputed ownership of their assets. The new technology also brings about exciting changes to the art world, but it may also fuel price bubbles that can damage the economic interests of these asset owners. In an exciting period of rapid change and emerging art and artists, it would be helpful for potential buyers to focus on the intrinsic value of the digital assets. Why should people find such assets desirable? The answer may be the beauty of a digital painting or the uniqueness of a digital display. One should try to form independent judgments of the value and try to stay away from herd mentality.

PART V

CONCLUSION

We don't always like changes. They bring about uncertainty. They call for more effort. They cause anxious feelings about the what-ifs. We particularly do not like them when we feel that they are being thrust upon us by external forces, that they may affect our lives significantly, or that they happen so fast that it is hard to catch up.

But changes pull us in like a magnet. Have you found yourself conversing with an AI chatbot, asking them everything from cocktail recipes to views on the stock market? Are you among the one in five adults in many countries who own cryptocurrencies as an adventurous personal investment? We are intrigued by changes as rational economic beings who maximize their utility and minimize their costs. We are always, knowingly or not, looking for better economic outcomes for ourselves. If there is a way to get more done for less, to have more of what we like and less of what we don't like, then we will take a shot at it.

Today's disruptive technologies represent such changes. And these changes are what motivated us to share the journey of this book together.

The purpose of this book is to offer some certainty of our future amid all the uncertainty. We started by laying out the basic workings of today's disruptive technologies and mapping out the important economic questions that will directly affect our personal well-being. While technologies are fast moving and take various shapes and forms, their economic impacts are often predictable by using well-established economic frameworks with reference to relevant past precedents and adjacent current events.

The most important thing I'd like you to take away from this book is that you will be fine—and your children will be too. The various technologies we have discussed in this book fall into one of two categories: they either represent a productivity-boosting tool that will help us accomplish more, or they represent a new form of money and wealth that complements the existing mainstream choices. As these technologies make their marks on the world, forces from the general public, regulators, and business communities are engaging in meaningful debates on how best to harness the power of these rather unfamiliar tools and deploy them effectively while protecting the interests of the public at large. Take comfort in the fact that past technological advancements such as the steam engine and mass production have all had their fair share of doomsayers at the time but have left the world a much better place. Just like today's disruptive technologies, those technologies were powerful and imperfect, but the world got together to steer the trajectory of history in the right direction.

The future is as bright as we make it. When faced with new developments, the most advisable course of action is to get to know them, understand how they can be constructively applied and intentionally abused, and be part of the changes that we want to see. The techonomic framework and the eighteen life-changing economic impacts that we have discussed in this book will hopefully serve as a handy guide for the future.

CONCLUSION

ENDNOTES

ENDNOTES

1 Brun-Schammé and Rey, 2021, *A new approach to skills mismatch,* https://www.strategie.gouv.fr/english-articles/new-approach-skills-mismatch

2 Accenture, 2023, *A new era of generative AI for everyone,* press document, https://www.accenture.com/content/dam/accenture/final/accenture-com/document/Accenture-A-New-Era-of-Generative-AI-for-Everyone.pdf

3 Goldman Sachs, 2023, *Generative AI could raise global GDP by 7%,* intelligence article hts://www.goldmansachs.com/intelligence/pages/generative-ai-could-raise-global-gdp-by-7-percent.html

4 Klein, K, 2006, *Is your team too big? Too small? What is the right number?,* Knowledge at Wharton, https://knowledge.wharton.upenn.edu/podcast/knowledge-at-wharton-podcast/is-your-team-too-big-too-small-whats-the-right-number-2/

5 Gartner, 2020, *Gartner Predicts 69% of Routine Work Currently Done by Managers will Be Fully Automated by 2024,* Press release, https://www.gartner.com/en/newsroom/press-releases/2020-01-23-gartner-predicts-69--of-routine-work-currently-done-b

6 Gartner, 2019, *Gartner Says 80 Percent of Today's Project Management Tasks Will Be Eliminated by 2030 as Artificial Intelligence Takes Over,* Press release, https://www.gartner.com/en/newsroom/press-releases/2019-03-20-gartner-says-80-percent-of-today-s-project-management

7 Deloitte, 2022, *Burnout is a current problem requiring long-term solutions,* Insights2Action, https://action.deloitte.com/insight/1568/burnout-is-a-current-problem-requiring-long-term-solutions

8 Shanafelt et al, 2022, *Changes in Burnout and Satisfaction with Work-Life Integration in Physicians During the First 2 Years of the COVID-19 Pandemic,* Mayo Clinic Proceedings, https://doi.org/10.1016/j.mayocp.2022.09.002

9 Sinsky et al, 2022, *COVID-Related Stress and Work Intentions in a Sample of US Health Care Workers,* Mayo Clinic Proceedings, https://doi.org/10.1016/j.mayocpiqo.2021.08.007

10 PwC, 2020, *Global Artificial Intelligence Study: Sizing the prize: Exploiting the AI revolution,* https://www.pwc.com/gx/en/issues/analytics/assets/pwc-ai-analysis-sizing-the-prize-report.pdf

11 International Trade Administration, 2023, *SelectUSA Software and Information Technology Industry,* Department of Commerce, USA, https://www.trade.gov/selectusa-software-and-information-technology-industry

12 Apple, 2023, *Job Creation,* https://www.apple.com/job-creation/

13 Federal Reserve, 2023, *Financial Accounts of the United States,* https://www.federalreserve.gov/releases/z1/20230608/html/recent_developments.htm

14 US Bureau of Economic Analysis, 2023, *Personal Income and Outlays,* https://www.bea.gov/data/income-saving/personal-income

15 Sawhill, Isabel V. et al, 2020, *Women's work boosts middle-class incomes but creates a family time squeeze that needs to be eased, Brookings,* Brookings Institution, *https://www.brookings.edu/articles/womens-work-boosts-middle-class-incomes-but-creates-a-family-time-squeeze-that-needs-to-be-eased/*

Made in the USA
Coppell, TX
05 March 2024

29798215R00142